HORACE'S ODES

and

The Mystery of Do-Re-Mi

STUART LYONS

Aris & Phillips is an imprint of
Oxbow Books, Park End Place, Oxford OX1 1HN

ISBN 978 0 85668 790 7   0 85668 790 1

A CIP record of this book is available from the British Library

The images of the Ode to Phyllis on the front cover and preliminary pages are taken from a fascimile in the third edition of Orellius's edition of Horace, volume II, published in Zurich in 1852, which is an accurate representation of the tenth-century original on ff.50–51 of the M425 codex of Horace in the Faculty of Medicine library at Montpellier in France.

Printed in Great Britain by
Short Run Press, Exeter

To Ellen

Felices ter et amplius
quos irrupta tenet copula nec malis
divulsus querimoniis
suprema citius solvet amor die.

Thrice happy those and more than thrice
Whom an unbroken love knot ties;
No harsh word will their true love fray
Until they reach their dying day.

Odes I. 13

Contents

Est michi nonum superantes annum

P lenus albani cadus. ~ est inhorto

P hylli nec tendis apium coronis. ~

E t hedere uis

M ultra. qua crines religata fulges;

R idet argento domus; ara castis

V incta uerbenis. ~ auet immolato

S pargier agno;

C uncta festinat manus huc atilluc,

C urscant mixte pueris puelle;

S ordidum flamme trepidant rotantes

V ertice fumum;

V t tamen nouis quibus aduoceris

G audiis idus tibi sunt agendae.

Ode to Phyllis from the M425 manuscript. Guido d'Arezzo used the melody to invent do-re-mi. Ths story is told in Chapter 3 and the music deciphered in Appendix II.

Acknowledgments

I would like to acknowledge my debt to Richard Andrewes of the Cambridge University Library music department for his help in deciphering the musical notation of the Ode to Phyllis in M425 and comparing it with the ut-re-mi melody used by Guido d'Arezzo.

I thank Iain Kerr for his help in recreating the Ode to Phyllis and Ann Rachlin for her support.

I wish to thank Professor Andrew Wallace-Hadrill, Director of the British School at Rome, for arranging my visit to the Auditorium of Maecenas and for his scholarly advice.

I renew my thanks to all those mentioned in my 1996 publication *The Fleeting Years*.

I am most grateful to my editor Clare Litt for her commitment to this project.

Above all, I thank my wife Ellen for her love and support. This book is dedicated to her.

Horace's Odes and the Mystery of Do-Re-Mi

1. Horace and the Augustan Age

When Horace died in 8 BC, he was confident he had built a lasting achievement. Fifteen years earlier he had written:

"I've made a monument to outlast bronze,
Rise higher than the pyramid of a king;
No gnawing rain, no north wind's violence
Or countless ranks of years and the fleeing
Of time could e'er this monument erase.
I shall not all die; some great part of me
Will escape Death's goddess. With posthumous praise
I'll freshly grow, be renewed constantly,
So long as priest with silent priestess shall
Climb upward to the Roman Capitol."

(III.30)

His prophecy was correct. Within a hundred years of his death, his odes were a standard text for study throughout the Roman Empire. Throughout Europe, until the end of the nineteenth century, there was barely a person of culture who could not quote passages from this master of the epigram and polished phrase. Today, when Latin is no longer a compulsory subject for matriculation and Classical Studies courses do not require classical languages, his brilliance is in danger of being lost.

As a young man, Horace was short, dark-haired and impetuous. In his middle age, the Roman head of state Augustus described him as "a most charming little fellow" and joked that he had watery eyes and was a most immaculate womaniser. In later life, Horace's hair turned white and he developed a voluminous girth. He was no aristocrat, but the son of a debt collector from a modest background who had made good. Through his wit, humanity and perception, and his prowess and artistry as a poet and entertainer, he attracted a devoted group of friends and admirers, and was welcomed in the highest circles of Augustan Rome.

His achievement was more than simply poetic, but one of extraordinary technical and cultural innovation:

"Humble, I rose to power
And I became the first of men to sing
Aeolian song transposed to Italian measures."

(III.30)

For Horace succeeded in translating Greek poetic form and metre into the more formal structures of Latin, creating a new strength and musicality. He was so fine a model, that later generations of Latin writers were unable to take his achievement forward.

He was born in Venusia in the province of Apulia on 8 December 65 BC, a year when Pompey the Great was the most powerful man in Rome, Crassus the richest, and Julius Caesar emerging as a young nobleman with a promising future. Within five years, the three had formed a political alliance known as the First Triumvirate, designed to provide stability in a republic constantly torn apart by the rivalry of different senatorial factions. Under their compact, they could each bring forward their legislative programmes to the Senate, and they were each awarded lucrative provinces to enrich them and keep them apart.

The rivalries could not be suppressed and the constitutional problem proved insurmountable. Stability in Italy depended on the consent of Rome's military leaders, who graduated from their civil consulships in Rome to proconsular duties as governors of Rome's subject provinces, to use their legions externally to protect Rome's interests and not internally to threaten Italy. When Julius Caesar crossed the Rubicon with his legions in 49 BC to protect, as he saw it, his position and honour, the Senate declared war. Although Caesar won the campaigns that followed, defeating Pompey in 48 BC and two of Pompey's sons in 45 BC, the civil wars did not end until his adopted son Octavian defeated Mark Antony in 31 BC at the Battle of Actium and agreed a constitutional settlement with the Senate three and a half years later. By this time, Horace was in his mid-thirties.

Horace's full name was Quintus Horatius Flaccus. His father was a freedman by rank and the name Flaccus has led to speculation about his origins. It is likely that either Flaccus senior's forebears had been slaves, probably coming from one of Rome's subject populations, or he had been taken captive in one of Rome's wars. After winning his freedom, he first became a debt collector and then a regional banker, and some of the language of finance appears in Horace's odes. Nothing is known of

Horace's mother or any siblings. As an infant he was looked after in the countryside by an Apulian nurse.

In Horace's writings, he tells us with pride and perhaps some embellishment that when he reached school age his father refused to enrol him in the local school in Venusia which the sons of the local military attended, as he did not want him to be looked down on by the sons of freeborn Romans. On the contrary, he wanted him to do better. The average Roman schoolboy was well drilled in the twelve times table, but not particularly literary. Flaccus wanted an aristocrat's education for his son. Although he only had a modest landholding, he took Horace to Rome to study under a respected teacher called Orbilius, kitting him out in smart clothes, employing servants to take him to and from school, and following his progress closely. The curriculum at Orbilius's school included Latin grammar, rhetoric, logic and literature enforced by regular beatings. The students read Homer's *Odyssey*, initially with the help of a third-century BC Latin verse translation by Livius Andronicus, which Orbilius declaimed. In later life, Horace noted he had thought Livius's choice of language somewhat inelegant.

By the time he reached his late teens, father and son agreed that Horace should go for further study to Athens, the centre of Mediterranean culture and learning. In Athens he will have continued to study rhetoric and advocacy, and attended philosophy lectures. He does not tell us when he was first introduced to the works of the Greek lyric poets. It is possible that his first exposure was in Rome under one of the many Greek grammarians who taught there. Certainly, his time in Athens will have given him a good grounding in the songs of Pindar, Alcaeus, Sappho and Anacreon, who had written their compositions five hundred years earlier.

Back in Rome, Julius Caesar had become supreme, to the dismay of his old enemies within the Senate, who seeing their power diminished accused him of an assault on Rome's ancient values. Brutus led the assassination of Caesar on the Ides of March 44 BC. Romans were soon bitterly divided between supporters and enemies of the *coup d'etat*. Horace and many of his student friends in Athens sided with Brutus, as a champion of the old republican constitution.

In the jockeying for power after the murder, Brutus, Mark Antony and Octavian, Caesar's adopted son and great-nephew, were the principal actors; Octavius, learning at the age of eighteen that he was Julius Caesar's principal heir, had assumed the name Caius Julius Caesar Octavianus. The Caesarian party, led by Antony and Octavian, took control of Italy through a vicious and widespread programme of murder euphemistically known as proscription. Brutus and his fellow conspirator Cassius left for the East. Cassius gathered an army in Syria; Brutus went to Athens where he formed a cadre of young officers. Horace was one of his recruits and was given the rank of military tribune, a junior officer on the general staff.

Brutus's army crossed to Ephesus and gathered more recruits in Asia Minor, before returning to northern Greece. Finally, in 42 BC, the assassins met the Caesarians on the battlefield of Philippi in Illyria. Two engagements took place; the second, after a three week interval, resulted in Brutus's defeat and suicide. Later, Horace recalled to a former comrade in arms the ignominy and trauma of the disaster:

> "With you I felt Philippi and swift flight,
>   Ingloriously leaving my small shield,
> When manliness was shattered and the might
>   Of youth fell chin-first on the shameful field."

(II.7)

Despite the Caesarian victory, the political fundamentals at Rome remained unchanged. Power lay not in the hands of the Senate or the aristocrats who sat there, but with those who could raise an army. After Philippi, a fresh rivalry surfaced, between Mark Antony and Octavian. In 40 BC their armies had a stand-off outside Brundisium, in south-east Italy. Octavian was saved from disaster by two factors: a young Antonian commander Asinius Pollio, subsequently honoured with Horace's Ode II.1, refused to attack him, and insisted on awaiting Antony's arrival; then, Caius Cilnius Maecenas, Octavian's friend and adviser, brokered an agreement under which Antony was to remain in the east, Octavian in the west, and a third Caesarian, Lepidus, in North Africa. To cement the Peace of Brundisium, Octavian's sister Octavia became Antony's bride. Thus, the Second Triumvirate was established.

Octavian had two principal aides. Marcus Agrippa, disciplined, effective and the apparent quintessence of Roman morality, was his general on both land and sea. Maecenas was his diplomatic negotiator and chief adviser. Maecenas's next assignment after Brundisium was to visit Sicily and try to reach an accommodation with Sextus Pompeius, a remaining son of Pompey the Great, with whom many of those threatened by the proscriptions had sought refuge. Pompeius had seized the islands of Sicily, Corsica and Sardinia. Having himself rid the Mediterranean of pirates, he was now characterised by the Caesarians as being as much pirate as hero. Octavian attempted to show his goodwill by marrying Scribonia, the sister of Pompeius's mother-in-law, in 40 BC. Maecenas's mission had some success and at the Peace of Puteoli in 39 BC the Triumvirate was enlarged to include Pompeius as a fourth partner.

Maecenas, though a Roman citizen, was an Etruscan by birth and a knight by rank, descended on his mother's side from the Cilnii, the original dynastic rulers of Aretium. He had a subtle mind, a broad cultural outlook, enormous wealth and an extravagant lifestyle. He enjoyed cultivating the company of young poets, and that is how he first met Horace.

Horace had returned to Rome under an amnesty after the defeat at Philippi. He was 23 years old and bought a position as a treasury clerk, for which his background suited him. In his spare time he wrote poetry. This brought him into contact with Virgil, Varius and Tibullus, and the first two introduced him to Maecenas in about 38 BC. The following year, Maecenas arranged for Virgil and Horace to travel with him to Brundisium, a zany journey by barge, mule and carriage described in Satires I.5. They made a trip of 230 miles in fifteen days, before Maecenas moved on to Tarentum to attend a conference with the Triumvirs.

Peace with Sextus Pompeius was short-lived. Octavian accused him of breaches of their agreements, divorced Scribonia and put together a navy to invade Sicily. A first attempt in 38 BC, when Agrippa was absent in Gaul, was a disaster. Pompeius attacked Octavian's home fleet as it sailed northwards through the Straits of Messina to join a second fleet from the Bay of Naples, and won an easy victory. As night fell, a storm blew up. The remains of Octavian's defeated fleet were shattered on the rocky capes of the Italian coast.

In the early summer of 36 BC, Octavian made a further attempt. He sailed south from Baiae with his navy, planning to co-ordinate an attack on Sicily with Antony, whose fleet was already waiting in the Straits, and a reluctant Lepidus. But as his navy was passing Cape Palinurus, there was another massive storm. The ships had thick timbers and lofty towers, so as to carry the largest possible number of marines and give them higher positions to fight from. This lack of mobility during the tempest led to the armada's destruction. The opposing fleet arrived. Those of Octavian's ships that were not set on fire or dragged away by the enemy were smashed against the rocks, and the men leapt overboard to save themselves.

The evidence that Horace was on board one of these ships lies in the poet's own words. Thanking his Muse for her protection, he writes:

"Dear to your springs and dancing, I
Survived the rout of Philippi,
The fall of the accursed tree,
Shipwreck and waves from Sicily."

(III.4)

The Latin words translated as "Shipwreck and waves from Sicily" are
"Sicula Palinurus unda": "Palinurus with the Sicilian wave". Palinurus is in
fact on the Tyrrhenian Sea. The term "Sicilian wave" makes sense if
Horace was with Octavian's navy at the time of the Palinurus disaster,
when the fleet's destination was indeed Sicily and the storm blew up from
the south. If Horace was indeed there, it is likely he would have been
accompanying Maecenas.

There are two other references to Palinurus in Graeco-Roman literature
that support the conjecture that Horace's shipwreck and Octavian's naval
defeat are interlocked. Dio Cassius, writing in Greek in his *Roman History*,
describes the incident and names the promontory. There is also an
intriguing reference in Virgil's *Aeneid*, the epic poem designed to legitimise
the Augustan Age. In Book Five, Virgil invents a helmsman called
Palinurus. As Aeneas approaches the cost of Italy for the first time,
Palinurus is overcome by sleep and falls overboard. Later, Aeneas meets
Palinurus's shade in the Underworld and is witness to a promise the Sibyl
makes to the dead sailor:

"Then neighbouring folk in cities far and wide,
Impelled by heavenly signs, will purge your bones,
And raise a mound and make grave offerings there,
And to the end of time the place will have
The name of Palinurus."

(Aeneid VI.378–381)

Perhaps the myth of Aeneas and the reality of Augustus (as Octavian was
later known) are on this occasion interchangeable. Could Virgil's purpose
have been to convert a naval disaster resulting from Octavian's
misjudgement into an Augustan myth in which the *pater patriae*, imbued
with heroism and piety, confronts a tragedy that is beyond his control to
prevent? Could it be that in the years after the disaster, the prophecy
invented by Virgil was not merely fulfilled but self-fulfilling, and that

annual ceremonies of purification and remembrance took place at Palinurus in honour of Octavian's dead?

Horace expects his audience to know about all three of his near-death experiences. Everyone knew about Philippi and he tells of his role in Odes II.7. He writes of the tree falling onto his head in II.13, a less funny event than some commentators have supposed, and mentions it again in III.8. He clearly assumes that his audience, not least his sponsor Maecenas, knows what happened at Palinurus, even though public discussion might have been taboo. It is surely more likely that Horace was shipwrecked there in the aftermath of Octavian's defeat at sea than at any other time. Indeed, there is no evidence for any other possibility.

The journey to Brundisium and the probable shared dangers at sea helped form a deep bond between Maecenas and Horace. Maecenas responded to Horace's poetic wit, *joie de vivre* and loyalty. Horace had a deep affection for Maecenas. Both were flattered and rewarded by their friendship, which went appreciably beyond the normal patron/client association. By the mid 30s Maecenas had provided Horace with capital and income for life through the gift of a country estate with five tenanted farms in the Sabine hills east of Rome.

In a continuation of the naval campaign of 36 BC, Octavian and Agrippa finally disposed of both Sextus Pompeius and Lepidus, the former executed with many of his noble adherents, the latter sent into exile. But the bounds of the Roman Republic were too narrow to contain the rivalry of Octavian and Antony. At first, there was an uneasy peace in which the Roman world was shared between them, with Antony taking the East, but soon Antony became passionately involved with Cleopatra, the Queen of Egypt. He divorced Octavia in 32 BC, signalling the end of his accord with Octavian. Rashly, he proposed to bequeath to Cleopatra and her sons territories over which Rome claimed rights. Octavian obtained a copy of his Will and this gave him both a *casus belli* and the support of the Senate. He drove Antony's supporters from Rome, and the Senate with diplomatic nicety declared war not against the Roman citizen, but against Cleopatra.

At the sea battle of Actium on 2 September 31 BC, Octavian had his victory. Antony and Cleopatra were defeated and fled to Alexandria, where first he and then she committed suicide:

"More fierce when she resolved to die,
Scorning a jailer's cruel galley,

No humble woman, she ne'er sank
     To grace a proud triumph, stripped of rank."
                                                    (I.37)

Maecenas had introduced Horace to Octavian some years earlier. Overwhelmed with work and in poor health, Octavian had wanted to steal Horace from Maecenas and offered him a position as private secretary. Horace declined. Octavian confirmed by letter that he was welcome to eat at his house. Maybe, he suggested, Horace would compose something on the victories of Agrippa. Horace penned a refusal, addressed tactfully to the distinguished general:

> "Too slight for such grand things, my sense of shame
>   And Muse that governs an unwarlike lyre
> Bar me from spoiling excellent Caesar's name
>   And yours with praise my talents can't inspire."

                                                    (I.6)

"I sing of parties," he continued, "of young girls who yearn/To fight their boyfriends with trimmed fingernails." His shame may have been simple modesty, a recognition that his talents lay elsewhere. Perhaps, too, he was still painfully aware of having been on the wrong side at Philippi.

                        *   *   *

Horace had begun his writing career not as a lyric poet, but as a satirist. Composing hexameters in a conversational style, he produced a series of witty, ribald discourses which he called *Sermones* or "Talks" and are known in English as the Satires. The first book was published in 35 BC and included poems on wealth, sex and friendship, as well as the journey to Brundisium. Five years later, the second book of Satires was published. Then, as Rome settled into a period of domestic peace, Horace put hexameter verse aside and turned to new rhythms based on Greek models. In 29 BC he published the seventeen Epodes, all but the last written in couplets with iambic or dactylic metres, where a longer verse is followed by a shorter. They were full of humour, satire and invective, and observations on love and politics, a mid-stage between his early hexameters and the polished lyric poetry of the Odes.

Although some odes were written earlier, it is the period between 29 BC and 23 BC, when the first three books of Odes were published, that marks the high point of Horace's creative development, just as it marks the consolidation of Octavian's position as head of the Roman state and the peak of Maecenas's career as his political adviser and urban administrator.

After his victory at Actium, Octavian spent 30 BC in the east, securing the frontiers of empire and the allegiance of the local populations and their rulers. In the summer of 29 BC, he returned to Rome a hero. On three successive days, at the invitation of the Senate, he led triumphal processions through the city in celebration of his victories. The Temple of Divine Julius was dedicated in honour of the dead dictator and with resonances for his heir. The following year, continuing to break with precedent, the Senate appointed Octavian consul for the fourth successive year since 31 BC and the sixth time in all. His prestige was enormous.

By the time the magnificent new Temple of Apollo was consecrated on the Palatine Hill in October 28 BC, an incautious observer might have asked who was the sun god, Apollo or Octavian. In an ode composed for the occasion, Horace confined himself to a more personal prayer:

> "Grant, o Latona's son,
>> That in sound health and, I pray,
>> With an unimpaired mind I may
> Enjoy the things I have won,
>
> And grant that I do not mar
>> Old age with dishonour, I pray,
>> And let me continue to play
> On the strings of my guitar."

(I.31)

Increasingly, Horace spent time on his country farm in the Sabine Hills above Tibur. The countryside, with its sounding springs, woodlands and rivers, was irresistible, and there was the farm itself, perched high in the hills, with a tall pine tree standing above the farmhouse (III.22), valleys and polished rocks below, and goats wandering all around (I.17). Why suppose, he asked,

"That I would want to build in the latest style
A hilltop palace with a swanky gate?
Why would I wish to change my Sabine vale
For riches that were more elaborate?"

(III.1)

Maecenas had a palace on the Esquiline Hill, but Horace inhabited a landscape where he could harvest the day (I.11) or lie in long grass under the shade of a poplar or pine, as a shimmering brook laboured below:

"Here, send for wine and perfumes sweet,
    The flowers of the rose soon dead.
While age and circumstance permit,
    And the three Fates spin their black thread!"

(II.3)

There were still ambiguities and stresses within the Roman republic that had to be resolved. On 13 January 27 BC, the first step was taken towards a constitutional settlement. Octavian restored the Senate and the People of Rome to their traditional places at the formal centre of the republic by resigning a number of his powers and overseas provinces to them. In return, on the proposal of Munatius Plancus, the Senate granted Octavian the title of Augustus. For each of the next five years, Augustus was awarded one of the two consulships, the highest civil office in Rome.

Horace now responded to the emergence of the Augustan Age and to the changing moral environment. In the Roman Odes, as the first six odes of Book III are known, he spoke out for a return to traditional values and patriotism. *"Dulce et decorum est pro patria mori,"* he declared (III.2). He praised the courage of Regulus who left Rome for certain torture rather than bring shame on it (III.5). The task for today's citizens was made clear:

"Roman, though guiltless, you must now atone
    For your forefathers' crimes, till you remake
The shrines and temples that are falling down
    And the images polluted with black smoke."

(III.6)

It would be simplistic to say that Horace had rejected the amoral hedonism of his earlier odes, for he continued to entertain his audiences with themes of love, drinking and the simple pleasures. But in his more formal utterances, he acknowledged the horror and futility of civil war, and supported the reinstatement of religious and moral values. In this, he anticipated, perhaps as a propagandist, the reforms in family law introduced a few years later:

> "He, who will end this impious age
> Of carnage and of civil rage,
> If he wants statues with the name
> 'Father of Cities,' may he tame
> Our unchecked immorality!"

(III.24)

Augustus had not lost his military appetite. He was no Alexander intent on foreign conquest for the sake of it, but was anxious to preserve peace within the empire by securing its borders and subduing dissident populations within. He left Italy within a year of being awarded his new title and spent three years away, first in Gaul and then Spain, where he fought a not entirely successful campaign against the Cantabrians in the north. He returned to Italy in the middle of 24 BC to find an atmosphere far more hostile than the euphoria of five years earlier.

There had been many Roman casualties in Spain. Augustus himself was ill and weak. There was disquiet among some of the old senatorial families about their loss of status. Augustus's annual consulships meant that half those who might have expected to gain high office and the subsequent lucrative provincial governorships were unable to do so. Now the leader expected his favourite nephew Marcellus to be made consul at the tender age of twenty-two. Matters reached a head when Marcus Primus, the governor of Macedonia, was accused of making war in Thrace without senatorial authority. He was brought to trial, where he was defended by Lucius Licinius Varro Murena, the brother of Maecenas's wife Terentia and half-brother of Proculeius (II.2). Murena, probably the person toasted by Horace in Odes III.19 on his appointment to the College of Augurs, had recently been appointed joint consul with Augustus. Despite reaching high office, he was hot-tempered and impetuous. He may or may not have been the Licinius whom Horace had warned:

> "Your life would be in better shape
> If you stopped pressing out to sea

Or clinging too close to the rocky cape
While eyeing storms too warily."

(II.10)

At Marcus Primus's trial Murena went on the offensive. He defended his client by accusing his fellow consul. Augustus and Marcellus, he claimed, had given his client authority to embark on hostilities. He underestimated Augustus's resolve. Augustus left his sick bed to deny the accusation. Primus was convicted.

During this trial of strength, Maecenas was guilty of a lapse of judgment. He warned his wife Terentia, widely believed to be the "Licymnia" of Odes II.12, that her brother's life was in danger. She passed the warning on. Murena was killed shortly thereafter. The regime put it about, correctly or incorrectly, that he had become involved in a murderous conspiracy organised by Fannius Caepio. Augustus's relationship with Maecenas never recovered.

Murena's consulship was passed to Calpurnius Piso, a former follower of Brutus and Cassius, in an endeavour to heal the divisions at Rome. Augustus's health broke down completely and, believing himself to be on the point of death, he handed his state papers to Piso and his signet ring to Agrippa. He recovered, attributing this to a regime of cold baths, whereupon he resigned his own consulate in favour Lucius Sestius. The crisis ended with a fresh constitutional settlement. Augustus gave up his annual consulships, but took on proconsular *imperium* across the empire and tribunician powers in government. There was tough talking within the Caesarian party, too. Agrippa's power increased, Marcellus moved into the background and Maecenas's fall was confirmed. His public position was taken over by Caius Sallustius Crispus, one of the few highborn addressees of a Horatian ode (II.2) who could justly have taken offence at its tone and content, particularly as his uncle had a reputation for embezzlement, venality and high spending.

Such was the background to the publication of the first three books of Horace's Odes late in 23 BC. Horace honoured Maecenas with the dedicatory prologue, Augustus with the second ode, and Virgil with the third. Lucius Sestius, the substitute consul, was given the Spring Ode, which began felicitously after the recent crisis:

"Keen winter melts, the pleasant time of spring
Has come in its due turn, the west wind blows."

(I.4)

Maecenas's political and social heyday was at an end. Horace lost position and prestige. During the three years from 23 to 20 BC, he returned to his hexameters and wrote the first book of Epistles, a collection of twenty poems of varying length. In the first of them Horace announced to Maecenas that he was giving up his lyric poetry. "My age and mind have changed," he declared (Epistles I.1.4). The Epistles reflect an easy philosophy of middle age, the security and comfort of the Sabine farm, and a concern about declining health and vigour. Then, from 20 BC Horace's poetic output almost ceased. His friends Virgil and Tibullus died. There was little for him to be enthusiastic about.

Augustus, however, remained an admirer. He liked Horace and, according to the historian Suetonius who had sight of his original letters, rated his compositions so highly that he believed they would last for ever. By 17 BC Augustus was head of a peaceful, well ordered empire. He decided to launch the Centennial Games, a showpiece event postponed five years earlier, which was designed to celebrate Rome's position as capital of the civilised world. The ceremonial and religious programme was to include a performance of a Centennial Hymn, and he appointed Horace to compose it.

This public recognition from the head of state and the opportunity to have his work performed in front of a large national and international audience was a high point in Horace's life. The *Carmen Saeculare* was a serious religious work, to be sung by a choir of freeborn Roman boys and girls, and it set out Rome's history, destiny and prayers in the context of the state religion.

After the Games, Augustus pressed Horace to add a fourth to his three books of Odes. He asked him to celebrate the victories of his stepsons Tiberius and Drusus over the Vindelici. Then, having read some of the Satires, he complained that no mention was made of him: "You must know I am angry with you," he wrote. "Are you afraid your future reputation will suffer because you were seen to be my close friend?" Horace succumbed. In 13 BC, he published his fourth and last book of Odes, a collection of fifteen pieces. Some of the freshness of expression had gone, but the craftsmanship remained, and in the last two odes he gave Augustus the desired recognition. A second book of Epistles emerged a short time later with its first poem addressed to Augustus. It was followed by the Epistle to Piso generally known as the *Ars Poetica*.

Horace died on 27 November 8 BC, in the year when Marcius Censorinus (the addressee of Odes IV.8) was consul with Asinius Gallus.

He was approaching his fifty-seventh birthday when he was struck by his final illness. The prophecy of Odes II.17 was fulfilled. Maecenas had predeceased him by two months, leaving most of his property, including the magnificent compound on the Esquiline Hill, to Augustus. Too weak to have a will prepared, Horace also named Augustus his heir. He was buried near Maecenas's tomb on the Esquiline Hill.

The epilogue to Book III may be regarded as Horace's formal epitaph. A philosophical epitaph is perhaps contained in the Ode to Postumus:

"Alas, the fleeting years slip by,
    And wrinkles and insistent age
Won't be delayed by piety;
    Nor death that no man can assuage ...

We must leave our house, the land we till,
    Our pleasing wife; of these trees you tend
None but the hated cypress will
    Follow their brief lord to the end."

Horace would not have been Horace without a sting in the tail. Adjusted to reflect twenty-first century drinking preferences, the ode ends:

"A worthier heir will quaff the wine
    That with a hundred keys you stored,
And stain the floor with port too fine
    To be served at a pontiff's board."

(II.14)

14

2. Horace the Songwriter

When we open our Latin text of Horace, the first words we see are *Carminum Liber Primus*: "Songs Book One." But in the English-speaking world we say "Odes." Through this persuasive definition, generations of readers have become conditioned to believing that Horace's *carmina* are poems, similar in nature, though more finely written, than the Epodes which preceded them.

Carmina: odes: poems. That's what almost every twentieth-century Latin teacher believed. Naturally, their students believed it too, as they cherry-picked their way through the texts and struggled through the syntax. They were more concerned to decipher Horace's compressed language than to ask about the musical references. If they did ask about Horace's lyre and cithara, their teachers put it all down to convention, as though Horace was an English romantic. When it came to understanding the genre, the academic establishment was sadly lacking in perfect pitch.

The popular odes students were given were in any case those where there was little or no musical vocabulary. The two Spring Odes (I.4 and IV.7), the ode to Pyrrha (I.5), the Soracte ode (I.9), the odes to Iccius (I.29), Dellius (II.3) Pompeius Varus (II.7) and Postumus (II.14), and the first Roman Ode (III.1) are among the finest poems in any language and among the first to be recommended to anyone wanting to discover Horace. But one of the consequences of limiting the student diet to them was that in the twentieth century people either forgot or never knew what Victorian scholars had discovered. Benjamin Jowett of Balliol College, Oxford, developed a sophisticated understanding of ancient music, but the Edwardians not only failed to build on his research, but largely ignored it. The late Enoch Powell, one of the finest classical scholars of his generation, was doing no more than expressing a common misapprehension when in an address to the Horatian Society in London he translated "*princeps Aeolium carmen ad Italos/deduxisse modos*" (III.30) as "The leader in converting Aeolian poetry into Italian diction."

Almost all the twentieth century commentators dismissed the possibility that Horace meant what he said. What he actually wrote was: "I shall be spoken of as the first person to have translated Aeolian song into Italian music." "*Carmen*" means "song", and "*modos*" means "measures" and is a term commonly used in early music to describe metre, melody, harmony and rhythm.

The evidence is inescapable. Let's start with Horace's *Carmen Saeculare*. One of the proudest events in Horace's life was the invitation he received

15

from Augustus to compose a hymn to Rome's gods for the Centennial Games of 17 BC. It was a huge national occasion, befitting Rome's status as the supreme power of the Mediterranean world.

The games were preceded by purification rights and the offering of first fruits. The opening ceremony took place at nightfall on 31 May. The games themselves ran on until 11 June on the authority of the *quindecimviri*, the college of priests of which Augustus and Agrippa were leaders. But the formal celebrations were from 31 May to 3 June. There were sporting events, theatrical performances of Greek and Latin plays, chariot races and even an animal hunt, all held within the context of the state religion.

Every evening Augustus made a public sacrifice, to the Fates, to Ilithyia the birth goddess and to the Earth Mother. On successive mornings he and Agrippa made a joint sacrifice, a bull to Jupiter and a beautiful cow to Juno. On the last morning of 3 June, they sacrificed to Apollo and Diana on the Palatine Hill. After the victim was slain, a choir of 27 boys and 27 girls, all freeborn and each of whose parents were alive, sang the *Carmen Saeculare*, first on the Palatine Hill and then on the Capitol:

> "Phoebus and mighty Diana holding sway
> Over the forests, heaven's bright ornament,
> Worshipped and worshipful, to our prayers consent
> On this holy day."

Even sceptics should agree that this is a hymn. There is a commemorative inscription confirming that Horace composed it: *"Carmen composuit Q Hor..ius Flaccus."* Yet one of the most respected twentieth-century Horatian scholars, Edward Fraenkel, wrote: "It is altogether unlikely that Horace, a non-musician, should have undertaken the arduous task of rehearsing and conducting the performance of a choir of amateurs," (*Horace*, 1957, pp 403–4). This is an extraordinary statement. Augustus had been thinking about this festival for a full five years. Is it really feasible that the head of state and of the Fifteen Men college of priests would have asked a writer who was musically illiterate and allowed a choir that could not sing to create and perform such an important political and religious showpiece?

Horace gives the lie to this proposition. Basking in his honour, he composed an Ode to Melpomene, the Muse of Lyric Song. It concludes:

> "Pierian Muse, you who instill
> Sweet sounds in the gold tortoiseshell,

Who even to the speechless fish
Will give a swan's voice if you wish,

This is all due to your bounty,
That passers-by now point at me,
The minstrel of the Roman lyre, –
I breathe and please, but you inspire!"

(IV.3)

This is not poetic convention. The tortoiseshell is the basic soundbox of the lyre, an inverted scooped-out shell to which horns, a crosspiece and strings were attached. Horace is *Romanae fidicen lyrae*, and *fidicen* means a person who plays on a stringed instrument. If anything is to be deduced from convention, it is that the Romans, who used Greece as the source of most of their literary and artistic culture, would have followed suit in the world of music.

According to myth, the tortoiseshell lyre was given by the god Mercury to Amphion of Thebes, as Horace notes (III.11). According to historical tradition, Terpander of Corinth converted the traditional four-stringed lyre to one of seven strings in about 650 BC, an innovation which led to the flowering of Greek lyric song. The fact that the Greek lyric poets – Pindar, Sappho, Alcaeus, Anacreon, Stesichorus and the rest – were musicians who sang their compositions is so well documented that it needs no further argument.

Sappho and Alcaeus, the models for Horace's Sapphic and Alcaic metres, flourished around 610 BC, but the guru of Greek musical theory was Pythagoras, who was born half a century later in about 558 BC. A native of the island of Samos, he had a golden birthmark on his thigh, which he said proved his descent from Apollo. As a precocious teenager, he was persuaded by Thales the natural scientist to visit Egypt to study mathematics and astrology. He spoke Phoenician as well as Greek, and when the Persian king Cambyses invaded Egypt in 525 BC, he moved on to Babylon where he studied music and metaphysics under a famous Chaldean teacher called Zaratas. After a brief return to Samos, he moved to Croton in Greek-speaking southern Italy, where he founded an academy for philosophical study and spiritual meditation.

Pythagoras's best known discovery was the geometrical theorem that still bears his name: in a right-angled triangle the square on the hypotenuse is equal to the sum of the squares on the other two sides. Probably, he

17

stole it from the Egyptians who used it to recalculate their landholdings after the annual Nile floods.

But he also had an almost religious belief in the Tectractys of the Decad or "Fourness of the Group of Ten." At this time Arabic numerals had not been invented. Numbers were designated by letters of the alphabet and their relationships were not easily understood. Pythagoras set out the number ten in an equilateral triangle that showed instantly that 1 + 2 + 3 + 4 = 10:

```
        *

      *   *

    *   *   *

  *   *   *   *
```

He discovered that the chief musical intervals could be expressed in simple numerical ratios involving these first four whole numbers. The octave was 2:1, the fifth was 3:2 and the fourth was 4:3. He saw that a fifth followed by a fourth made an octave, but that the two ratios had to be multiplied rather than added to produce the correct result. He saw that a tone was a fifth less a fourth, but that the interval had to be calculated by dividing the larger ratio by the smaller. If the pitch for the middle string of a lyre could be fixed by a tuning instrument, the other tones could be tuned from it.

The musical culture of early Greece was fragmented and diverse until Pythagoras revolutionised the theory of music. Communities had different tribal origins and were separated by mountains or sea or both. They spoke Greek in different dialects. They tuned their lyres in different ways. The Myxolydian, Lydian and Phrygian regions of Asia Minor, and the Dorian region of mainland Greece did not put their tones and semitones in a uniform sequence. Musicians sometimes even tuned their strings with quarter-tone intervals. But by the end of the fifth century BC, the Greeks had a shared theoretical framework for musical analysis. Although their system included chromatic and enharmonic scales, the principal type of musical scale was diatonic. It was based on the four-note tetrachord, which sounded like the opening notes of the Londonderry Air, "O Dan-ny Boy", with intervals of 1/2 1 and 1 respectively, like today's notes of E F G A. To form a full length scale, one added a higher tetrachord to a lower. Just as a tetrachord normally contained two and a half tones of intervals, so an eight-note scale had seven intervals of five full tones and two semitones.

As a student in Athens Horace was living in a society where every free-born child was expected to play the lyre and sing the songs of the old lyric bards. The musical ethos of 400 BC was still strong in 43 BC. "They make the rhythms and melodies take root in the children's minds," Plato had written (*Laws* 812d) and he classified four different harmonies in *The Republic*. Students were expected to be proficient in seven diatonic scales, each of which started on a separate note and created a different mood. Aristophanes wrote that Athenian children not only played in the Dorian mode, which was regarded in Athens as the most balanced and sociable of all the modes, but could be kicked out of class if they were unable to re-tune their lyres or citharas for the other modes. Aristotle described the Phrygian mode as "divinely suffused", perhaps implying that it was too oriental for his taste. Names which had formerly been regional now came to denote different modes based on the different starting pitch of the tetrachord and the different intervals between the notes.

1. Mixolydian	½	1	1	½	1	1	1
2. Lydian	1	1	½	1	1	1	½
3. Phrygian	1	½	1	1	1	½	1
4. Dorian	½	1	1	1	½	1	1
5. Hypolydian	1	1	1	½	1	1	½
6. Hypophrygian	1	1	½	1	1	½	1
7. Hypodorian	1	½	1	1	½	1	1

Horace was aware of these distinctions, as the following lines signify:

"The lyre and pipes will play their combined ode,
  One in the Dorian, one in foreign mode."

(Epodes IX.5–6)

Pythagoras was the son of Panthous. When Horace writes of Panthoides being called twice to the underworld (I.28), he is referring to Pythagoras's belief that, in a previous incarnation, he had been Euphorbus, a warrior in the Trojan War. The subject of this ode is Archytas. Who was he and why did Horace choose to commemorate his murder on a lonely Italian beach?

"Archytas, you once measured sea and land
    And the numberless sand;
Now by the Matine shore your slight reward must
    Be a handful of dust."

Archytas came from Tarentum and lived between about 400 and 350 BC. He was a teacher at the Pythagorean School at Croton. He was a mathematician, musical theorist and acoustic scientist. Like his fellow Pythagoreans, he believed that an understanding of numbers was fundamental to the understanding of the physical world. One of his preoccupations was to solve the problem of doubling the cube. He drew a three-dimensional model, from which he drew conclusions about continued proportions. He applied his theory to musical harmony and created a new version of the enharmonic tetrachord through a mathematical variation from the Pythagorean method. He asserted that sound was caused only when there was some kind of impact between one body and another and when motion was involved. In this imperfect theory, there were the beginnings of ideas about sound waves.

Archytas was a little known figure in Horace's Rome. His murder, it is true, had taken place not far from Horace's birthplace. But that was over three hundred years earlier. It is hard to believe that Horace would have been stimulated to write about it, unless he had more than a passing interest in musical theory.

Horace knew his music. In the Epodes, to use his own words, his aim was to "*scribere versiculos*," to write little verses. In the odes, he wrote songs. As he notes in the Epistles:

> "How can I be thought capable here, amid the billows of business and the tempests of the city, of composing lines to awake the sound of the lyre?"
>
> (Epistles II.2)

Music resonates throughout the Odes, because they are *carmina*. The rocks of Ustica echo to the sound of pipes, as Tyndaris plays a lyre from Anacreon's birthplace of Teos (I.17). The end of III.3 and the beginning of III.4 restate the musical message: "Great themes with poor music you diminish" leads into "Pluck Phoebus' strings, play his guitar."

From the start of Book I, his references to music and musical instruments are so specific that it would be perverse not to take him at his word. Sometimes he mentions the lyre, sometimes the barbiton, a smaller instrument more like a lute (I.32; III.26). Often, he plays and writes of the cithara. He writes:

> "Without you, sweet Pimplean Muse, the renown
> I confer profits nothing, so let honours come
> With new-fangled strings and a Lesbian plectrum."
>
> (I.26)

"You enjoy songs, and songs I can create," he says (IV.8). In the next ode he declares, "*Verba loquor socianda chordis*":

> "Lest you may think my words will die,
> Which by arts ne'er divulged before,
> Born by the resonant Aufidus, I
> Join to the chords of my guitar ..."
>
> (IV.9)

In Book IV, there is a *carmen* to Apollo, the god of music, which turns remarkably into a rehearsal for the *Carmen Saeculare* itself. Suddenly, two-thirds of the way through the hymn, the boys and girls of Horace's choir are at centre stage, as Horace taps out the Sapphic metre:

> "Phoebus has given me his inspiration,
> Phoebus the art of song, a poet's name:
> O girls who are the first girls of the nation,
> And boys who come from fathers of fair fame,
>
> Wards of Delos' goddess, to whose bow fleeting
> Lynxes and antelopes meekly succumb,
> Keep to the Sapphic metre and the beating –
> Observe the rhythmic beating of my thumb."
>
> (IV.6)

If any doubt remains that Horace is making music, it is dispelled in the last stanza:

"When you are wed, you'll say, "For the gods above,
    When the new century brought festive days,
I once performed a song that they might love,
    And learned the music of the bard Horace!"

(IV.6)

The poet Ovid confirms it. In exile early in the first century AD, he remarks that Horace's music has reached the shores of the Black Sea: "Horace with his numbers captivates our ears, as he strikes up his elegant songs on the Roman lyre," (*Tristia* IV.10.49–50). The term "numbers" has been used throughout the centuries to refer to songs in performance.

With or without music, the Odes would be recognized as a collection of the highest order, but the musical settings give clarity and articulation to Horace's marriage of Latin syntax with the rhythms of the lyric composers of Greece, and make sense of language in the *carmina* whose meaning has been drowned out by false assumptions. Here is Horace writing an ode to his sponsor Maecenas, who is toying with the idea of composing an epic song on Rome's past victories:

"The long and fierce Numantian war,
    Rough Hannibal and Punic blood
    Reddening the Sea of Sicily should
Not be themes for a soft guitar ...

No, not such themes; but you should write
    A prose account ...

My Muse has asked that I should tell
    Of sweet-singing Licymnia."

(II.12)

The Latin is specific: *nolis longa ferae bella Numantiae | ...mollibus aptari citharae modis"* – "You should not try to fit the long and fierce Numantian wars ... to the soft music of a cithara ... You should write a prose history of Augustus's wars ... My Muse wants me to tell of the sweet songs of lady Licymnia."

The realisation that Horace is not just a poet but a songwriter illuminates the entire corpus. The final lines of his dedication to Maecenas take on fresh point and clarity:

"The woodlands cool,
And Nymphs and Satyrs dancing with light grace,
Divide me from the ordinary race
Of men, if Muse Euterpe plays the flute
And Polyhymnia tunes the Lesbian lute;
But if you count me among the lyric bards,
My head will be so high, I'll hit the stars."

(I.1)

The phrase Horace uses is *lyricis vatibus*: not lyric in our modern sense, but "of the lyre".

Clearly, Horace was regularly involved in some form of theatrical performance. Indeed, he uses precise vocabulary to convey an image of himself being summoned on stage with his barbiton:

"We're called. If ever, sitting in the shade,
I've strummed a tune with you that, both this year
And in the years to come, will still be played,
Come, sing a Latin song, o Grecian lyre."

(I.32)

In spite of the opening "We", this was a solo performance, for the other party is the Grecian lyre. Some odes require more than one voice. The Hymn to Apollo and Diana (I.21) needs a small mixed choir. Archytas and the Sailor (I.28) calls for two male voices. The Drinking Party (I.27) has at least two voices. The Love Duet (III.9) has one male and one female voice. These examples point to different kinds of performance at different venues, some connected with religious worship and others at private entertainments ranging from performances at Augustus's court to drinking parties with expatriate Greeks. The most natural venue, however, must have been the palace of Horace's patron.

Maecenas's residence in Rome was set in a magnificent gardened compound on the Esquiline Hill. There he built his "hill-top palace with a swanky gate," a "mansion climbing to the sky" from which he could "stare at the city smoke and gaze/At blessed Rome's wealth and noisy ways." In about 30 BC he built what is now called the Auditorium of Maecenas, a single-storey hall, half sunken into the ground, about 24 metres long and 11 metres wide. The building was discovered in 1874. Its two side walls and the rear wall are rectilinear, but the short wall at the far end of the interior is a semicircular apse fronted by seven tiers of marble steps. A graffito written on an external wall echoes some lines of the Greek poet Callimachus, asking pardon for bad behaviour brought on by wine and love.

At first scholars assumed this was a theatre, with tiered seating in the apse. A more detailed examination of the pipework and plumbing now suggest that the marbled apse formed a backdrop for an elegant water feature, whose gently cascading flow cooled the atmosphere and enhanced the acoustics. Above this cascade were five niches decorated with *trompe l'oeil* frescoes, giving the impression of a beautiful garden. There were six more niches along each of the two side walls, which may have housed a collection of statues. The hall seems to have been an elaborate dining salon, a sort of aquatic fairyland or *nymphaeum*, where guests at a *symposium* could recline on their *triclinium* couches and enjoy food, drink and entertainment.

After Maecenas's death, the property passed to Augustus. It was redecorated in 2 AD on the return of Tiberius from Rhodes, and subjected to minor structural change in the reign of Nero. But when Maecenas was in his pomp, this was a setting which makes sense of what to modern ears can be disturbing contrasts in Horace's songs. Here, the bawdy, drunken, moralistic, warm, tolerant and wise elements could live together. As an evening's revelry progressed, the "good odes" admired by Victorian schoolmasters could be followed without detriment by the "bad odes" criticised in Lempriere's Classical Dictionary of 1788: "The poetry of Horace, so much commended for its elegance and sweetness, is deservedly censured for the licentious expressions and indelicate thoughts which he too frequently introduces." Horace was not a gentle English romantic who went off the rails. He was poet of consummate craft, who set his work to music and entertained the Roman aristocracy with his songs.

In 1930, the German musical historian Guido Adler reported he was aware of melodies for six of Horace's odes. The first five he mentions are for the Dedication to Maecenas (I.1), Virgil's trip to Athens (I.3), the Ode to Tibullus (I.33), the Love Duet (III.9), and the Bandusian Spring (III.13). Only fragments survive in a handful of medieval manuscripts and there can be no certainty that any of them is an original tune from Horace's time. Indeed, it would be surprising if they were. There are very few melodies in the history of song that have enjoyed the longevity of Greensleaves. There was no system for keeping musical records in the Roman Empire which could have enabled the music of the Augustan Age to survive. Nevertheless, these fragments confirm the existence of a Horatian musical tradition and its survival through the Dark Ages in some of the courts and monasteries of Europe.

The most extensive surviving melody is for the Ode to Phyllis (IV.11): *Est mihi nonum superantis annum.* A Benedictine monk used this setting more than a thousand years after Horace's death to create the sounds and sequence of do-re-mi. He used this innovation as a memory device to help his choristers recall the correct pitches for their notes. The story of Horace, Guido d'Arezzo and the do-re-mi mystery is about to be unravelled.

3. Guido d'Arezzo and the Do-re-mi Mystery

Suppose you were appearing on *Who Wants to be a Millionnaire?* and the quizmaster gave you this multiple choice question:

> Where did the original music for do-re-mi come from?
> Was it:
> (a) A musical by Rodgers and Hammerstein?
> (b) A letter from Guido d'Arezzo?
> (c) A hymn by Paul the Deacon?
> (d) An ode of Horace?

There is a lot at stake. You aren't sure of the answer and you decide to ask the audience. What would be their likely answer? Most would probably choose Rodgers and Hammerstein, the writers of the musical *The Sound of Music.*

> "Doh, a deer, a female deer,
> Re, a drop of golden sun,
> Mi, a name I call myself ..."

It is an unforgettable melody. It is also what is known as a mnemonic, or memory device. Each line begins one note higher than the preceding line, and if you remember the tune, you remember the relationships of the musical scale.

If you were more scholarly or better informed, you would think of Guido d'Arezzo, the eleventh century Benedictine monk who invented the musical stave and the do-re-mi "solmization" system. You would feel certain that your answer was correct, and there is a chance the person who set the question would agree with you. But you and the researcher would both be wrong. Guido found the original do-re-mi music and used it, but he did not compose it.

If you were very well versed in musical history and the sort of person who goes for an answer that is just a little bit too clever, you might choose Paul the Deacon, the eighth-century cleric and historian. There might be a recollection of something you had once read stored at the back of your mind. Didn't the words to do-re-mi come from a hymn Paul had written to celebrate John the Baptist? Wasn't that what Guido borrowed two hundred years later? The truth, however, is that Paul the Deacon wrote only the words, not the music.

You would almost certainly reject the last option: an ode of Horace. You would be in good company. But that is the correct answer. The tune came from Horace's Ode to Phyllis (IV.11). This is not to say that Horace himself wrote the melody, for it takes a lot for any tune to survive a thousand years. But the melody to which the Ode to Phyllis was sung in the tenth and early eleventh centuries AD is the melody that Guido used for his invention.

What were the connections between Guido d'Arezzo, Paul the Deacon, and Horace's Ode to Phyllis, and why have they been hidden in mystery for so long? How, where and why did Guido find the music? There is no evidence that before he put the tune and words together they had belonged in any sense to one another. The answer lies in a little known tenth-century manuscript in a French medical school library.

But first, who was Guido d'Arezzo and what made him come up with his remarkable do-re-mi invention? He was born in the 990s and began his career as a young monk at Pomposa, an isolated Benedictine monastery on the Adriatic coast of Italy some thirty miles north of Ravenna. The monastery had been given independence from the Archbishopric of Ravenna in 1001, and this freedom launched it on a fifty year period of brilliance. Its uniqueness lay partly in its successful combination of two types of monks in the Benedictine tradition, the cenobites who lived in the institution, serving under the Rule and an abbot, and the eremites who lived as recluses and hermits. At Pomposa, both practices were welcomed and integrated under Abbot Guido degli Strambiati, a leader of scholarly asceticism, who presided over a remarkable flowering of talent from 1011 to 1046.

Guido d'Arezzo was a young music scholar of exceptional talent, who clashed with the established monks because of his insistence on new methods of music-teaching. The older monks held that musical harmony was given by God. To tamper with the time-honoured methods of teaching Gregorian chant was sacrilegious and to persist in changing them put individual pride above community commitment. They accused Guido of heterodoxy and pride. Guido felt the atmosphere "so choked by the snares of the envious, that you can scarcely breathe." In the interests of harmony, Abbot Guido degli Strambiati dismissed him from the monastery but found a position for him in Arezzo, the capital of Etruria which had been Maecenas's birthplace over a thousand years earlier.

Guido was in his early twenties. His confidence shaken, he presented himself to Bishop Theodaldus. Theodaldus, dynamic and commercial, saw an opportunity and appointed Guido head of the cathedral choir school.

Up to that date, choristers had learned their music by rote. There was no written sheet music. There was no piano keyboard with black and white notes to help their understanding. The only musical notation was in the form of small neumes or signs over a written text. Guido used a monochord to teach the notes and intervals. He explained the modes. He extended the musical range to a gamut of twenty-one notes. He taught his pupils to divide the monochord into notes in five easy steps.

In rehearsal he would guide his choristers by pointing to the four fingers of his left hand or the spaces in between. Later, he decided to transpose the fingers and spaces onto written staves, explaining that notes on the same line or space always made the same sound. They might be faster or slower, but the pitch never changed. To emphasise the point, he coloured the C row yellow and the F row red.

Having taught them the intervals, he moved to rhythm. He taught that chants should be metrical. He compared them with the verses written by the lyric poets of old. He made the choristers beat time to them. He taught them dactyls, spondees and iambics, tetrameters, pentameters and hexameters. At the end of a phrase, he said, the notes should be more widely spaced: "It's like a horse that has been galloping and comes to a break rather exhausted."

Guido's lessons were full of examples and illustrations. He drew this diagram for his students:

<u>Music is the movement of Notes</u>

<u>Tone</u>   <u>semitone</u>   <u>major third</u>   <u>lesser third</u>   <u>fourth</u>   <u>fifth</u>

ASCENT   DESCENT
(arsis)   (thesis)

Notes are joined

ONE TO ANOTHER   ITSELF TO ITSELF

similarly   dissimilarly
                                      according to the various qualities
one placed above another   of depth
one placed below another   and of height
one placed between others   of increasing
one placed next to another   and decreasing
mixed   intervals

"Anything that is spoken," he said, "can be made into music." He played a game with his class that inched him towards the invention of do-re-mi.

"Let's take the five vowels," he said. "As they bring euphony to words, maybe they will bring harmony to neumes. Let's put them one by one under the letters of the monochord, and as there are only five of them, let's keep repeating them." Then he wrote:

G A B C D E F G a *b* c d e f g a
a e i o u a e i o u a e i o u a

"Think about this arrangement. As all speech is set in motion by these five letters, let's see if we can activate five notes. Let's take any phrase and add to its syllables the musical notes that are next to the vowels. Then let's sing them as they are written here. '*Sancte Johannes, meritorum tuorum copias nequeo digne canere*' – 'St John, I cannot sing worthily of the abundance of your merits.' "

29

G	u			rum tu-	rum		
F	o	Jo-	to-	o-	co-		o
E	i		ri-		pi-		dig-
D	e	cte	-nes me-			neque-	ne nere
C	a	San-	han-		as		ca-

Then he started again, but this time he placed two lines of vowels under the notes, so that his pupils could have greater flexibility to choose a setting that conformed with the rules of modes, ascents and descents.

G	A	B	C	D	E	F	G	a	*b*	c	d	e	f	g	a
a	e	i	o	u	a	e	i	o	u	a	e	i	o	u	a
o	u	a	e	i	o	u	a	e	i	o	u	a	e	i	o

It was the first recorded theory of melody writing in the western musical tradition.

Guido set out his teaching system in a book called the *Micrologus* and dedicated it to his bishop Theodaldus: "Guido, would that he were the least of your monks," he wrote. "While my desire is to pursue at least a modicum of the solitary life, Your Gracious Eminence required my humble participation in the study of the Holy Word."

He added: "It is marvellous that the boys of your church should do better in the practice of music than experienced men everywhere else." A final remark bore witness to the wounds of the past and his continuing insecurity: "I have not concerned myself with those who might go blue with annoyance if the training of others went well."

Guido's choristers had mastered in days what had taken weeks to learn previously. They sang with perfect pitch and built an impressive repertoire, filling the cathedral with worshippers. Arezzo was a bustling commercial centre, where religious tourism was big business. The city competed with Florence and Perugia for the revenues of pilgrims bound for Rome. Bishop Theodaldus was able to add side chapels to the cathedral and to commission a new church to St Donat. Artisans, stallholders and the chapel custodians, who charged visitors for bread and candles, and then recycled them for further sale, all profited.

By 1028, Guido's reputation had reached Rome and he was summoned to an audience with Pope John XIX. English historians recognise John XIX as the pontiff to whom King Canute bent the knee and paid a large fee for the privilege of developing the Church in England. John's Roman contemporaries saw him as the only man to have risen from layman to pontiff in a single day, the former Count Romanus of Tusculum who used the proceeds of corruption to buy the papacy on the death of his brother Benedict VIII. But to Guido, the Pope was the successor of St Peter the Apostle, the rock on which the Church was built and the holder of the keys to the kingdom of heaven. Highly strung, full of apprehension and troubled with a weak chest, Guido made the journey with two companions, Prior Peter of Arezzo and Abbot Grunwald of Badacroce, arriving in Rome at the height of August.

The audience was successful for as long as it lasted. When Guido presented his antiphoner, Pope John was enthralled by the staves, lines, spaces and colours, and demanded a singing lesson: "You must teach me a verse I have never heard before, so I can sing it perfectly." Guido complied, the Pope was thrilled, but the audience came to an abrupt end. The heat and the occasion made Guido ill. His lungs heaved from the stench of the city's marshes. Nonetheless, he had gained the recognition and reassurance he yearned for, and it was agreed he would return that winter to make a presentation to the papal court.

A second event occurred to boost his confidence. He visited his former abbot Guido degli Strambiati, who tried the antiphoner and was convinced by the musical innovations, begging his former novice to return to Pomposa: "A monastery is where you belong, not a bishop's house." Guido d'Arezzo declined. He returned to Arezzo with fresh enthusiasm and searched for the final element in his teaching system, a mnemonic for the notes and intervals of the musical scale.

At last he found what he was looking for. How and where, he never revealed. But he announced his discovery to his old friend Michael of Pomposa in his *Letter concerning an Unknown Song*, which must have been written before the Pope's death on 20 October 1032, as the letter mentions Pope John as still living. Guido wrote:

> "Either the times are hard or God's judgments are obscure, when truth is trampled on by lies, and love is trampled on by envy ... I have been moved by divinely inspired charity to make available to you and as many others as possible, as quickly and as carefully as I can, a favour granted me by God, although I am the most unworthy of men ... Here is an easy and tested way of learning an unknown melody ... If you want to commit a note to memory ... concentrate on the same note at the beginning of a tune you know particularly

well. Let it be this tune, which I use from beginning to end when I teach my boys."

Then he wrote down some words. They came from the first stanza of a poem in praise of St John the Baptist which Paul the Deacon had written at the end of the eighth century. Paul was born into a noble Lombard family in about 720 and became a Benedictine monk, teaching and writing history at the court of the Duke of Benevento. At the end of his career, he retired to the great monastery of Monte Cassino, where he stayed until his death in about 799. One of his pastimes was to write Latin verses, and he wrote the poem shortly before he died. It is set out in the Concise Oxford History of Music thus:

"*ut queant laxis*
resonare fibris
mira gestorum
famuli tuorum
solve polluti
labi reatum
sancte Johannes."

("In order that, with loosened fibres, your servants may be able to sing again the wonders of your deeds, absolve the guilt of our polluted lip, holy St John.")

The first two letters of the initial words of each phrase or half line became the words of Guido d'Arezzo's musical mnemonic: *ut – re – mi – fa – sol – la*, later known as Guido's hexachord. *Ut* is still often used on the continent, and was common in England until the late-eighteenth century and beyond, when the first and last notes of the scale became *do*, probably derived from the Latin *dominus*. When the hexachord was eventually extended to the octave, it seems that **si** was named for the initial letters of *sancte Iohannes* and later became *ti*.

Guido carefully set out the poem in his letter to Michael. Above the words, he wrote down some musical notation. The effect was that each phrase started one note higher than its predecessor in the hexachord:

C   D F DE D   D D C D E E

Ut que-ant la-xis   Re-so-na-re fi-bris

32

```
EEG E D EC D      F   G A G FED D
Mi-- ra ge-sto-rum   Fa-mu-li tu-o---rum

GAG F E   F GD   A G A F GA A     GF D   C E   D
Sol- ve pol-lu-uti   La-bi-i re-a--tum,   san-cte Jo-an-nes!
```

"Don't you see," he continued, "how the six phrases each begin with a different note? If you have learned as I explain and know the beginning of each phrase so that you can start any one you want without hesitation, you will be able to sing these six notes properly whenever you see them."

This is how the tonic sol-fa solmization system was born. It was the second time St John had featured in his recorded teaching. But the melody was not in any of the hymn collections of the time. And Guido never revealed the source of the music. To find out why he was so secretive, we must travel to Montpellier in the south of France.

*   *   *

The School of Medicine at Montpellier University was established in 1795 on the site of a 14th century Benedictine monastery. It is a long, austere, three-storey building with a stone-clad facade. Inside, the hallway is large and cold. A wide, stone staircase curves to the upper floors, where there is a nondescript library. This is the home of a small collection of medieval books that came to Montpellier in 1804.

Napoleon had recently assumed office as First Consul of France. He was determined to confiscate from religious foundations and the estates of émigré aristocrats any "literary deposits" that could be regarded as part of the National Heritage. His principal agent was his Minister of the Interior Jean-Antoine Chaptal, a distinguished industrial scientist and professor of chemistry at Montpellier University. Although ennobled by Louis XVI as the Count of Chanteloup, Chaptal had been a committed supporter of the French Revolution and in the 1790s directed the revolutionary government's production of gunpowder. Now he chose a medical student and part-time librarian at the School of Health to lead the work of confiscation, a solid and persistent young man called Gabriel Prunelle. In April 1804, after a tour across northern France with three assistants, Prunelle found a collection of manuscripts in the Oratory library at Troyes.

The books had been assembled in the sixteenth century by Pierre Pithou, a scholar and publisher, whose principal business was to buy rare manuscripts and to re-print and re-issue them. He must have been a significant figure in Troyes, for a street there is still named after him. One of the books in the Pithou collection was a codex of the works of Horace.

Prunelle took the Horace, together with several other codices, back to the medical library at Montpellier. Known to scholars as M425, its label in fact reads H425. A bookplate from the Oratory at Troyes is still in place inside the front cover. The book is about eight inches high and five and three-quarter inches across, and has been rebound in worn boards with a splitting spine. It consists of a manuscript version of the complete works of Horace on folded quarto vellum pages. The text is handwritten in a script known as Carolingian minuscule.

The emperor Charlemagne is credited with providing the stimulus for Carolingian minuscule. He wanted to see a European writing standard developed, so that the educated classes could read the Roman alphabet in a common form. To this end, he sent for the English scholar, Alcuin of York, who ran the palace school and scriptorium at Aachen for most of the period from 782 to 796. Alcuin introduced a clear, uniform and legible lower-case script with disciplined rounded shapes, clear capital letters where needed, and spaces between the words. The script took hold in France and Germany from 800 to 1200, but met some resistance in Italy. Manuscripts written during this period can be dated with reasonable precision because of the way the script developed.

On the fiftieth folio of the codex is the Ode to Phyllis (IV.11). Horace wrote the ode when he was about fifty years old. The song tells of how Horace and Phyllis are preparing a birthday party for Maecenas. Perhaps the party is in substitution for the *symposium* which Maecenas can no longer host or attend, and the references to Phaethon and Bellerophon may have as much to do with Maecenas's own fall from grace, as with Horace's advice to Phyllis. It is one of the most beautiful of all Horace's songs, sparkling with warmth, love and grace. It begins:

> "I've a full flask of Alban wine,
>   Phyllis, that's nine years old and more;
> My garden has parsley you can twine
>   For garlands, and a mighty store

Of ivy to bind your shining hair.
The silver smiles within my home;
Chaste vervain covers my old altar
That craves the sacrifice of a lamb."

(IV.11)

The Latin text in M425, complete with the scribe's errors, reads:

》》

A D P H I LL I D E M

》》》

Est michi nonum superantis annum
Plenus albani cadus. – est inhorto
Phylli nec tendis apium coronis. –
Est hedere uis

Multa. qua crines religata fulges;
Ridet argento domus; ara castis
Vincta uerbenis. – auet immolato
Spargier agno;

It is clear from the transcription errors of *michi* for *mihi* ('to me'), *inhorto* for
in horto ('in the garden'), and the nonsensical *nec tendis* ('nor do you stretch
out') for *nectendis* ('suitable for binding'), that this is a mechanical copy of an
earlier manuscript, rather than a revised or freshly edited version. The
regularity of the script, the long letter 's', the simple ascenders and the
ligature 'ft' for 'st', suggest it may have been written around 950, although
this needs to be verified by experts. Above each line is musical notation, a
succession of strokes and dots at various heights to indicate the rise and
fall of the melody. The scribe has deliberately left ample spaces between
each of the verses of the first six stanzas, so as to accommodate his
neumes. The fact that the scribe laid out the text so punctiliously for this
purpose adds to the circumstantial evidence that the melody truly belonged
to the ode and was not some casual interpolation.

These so-called Latin neumes (named from the Greek *neuma* meaning a
sign or nod) are not just contemporary with the handwritten Carolingian
minuscule text, but by the same hand. They are certainly not later additions
to the text that could have been made in Guido's time or subsequently and
they add a further clue as to the dating and origin of the manuscript.

Neumes were introduced in the middle of the ninth century and were widely used in tenth-century France, but hardly at all in Italy. Sometimes they take the form of dots, sometimes of extended accents. Generally, they denote upward or downward changes in pitch, and occasionally they indicate rhythm through denoting brevity or length.

The markings over the first two verses of the first stanza are not too clear. The rope design beneath the title "AD PHILLIDEM" and the large dark initial *"E"* of *"Est"* conceal some of the notation. The reader's eye is drawn to the second stanza where the neumes are clear. Musical scholars can still read them today. Neumes do not give the names of pitches or denote the precise relationship of the tones and semitones, but are "diastematic." Indeed, that is the precise limitation Guido was seeking to correct. If, however, the tune is set at the right starting pitch, the melodic line can be followed with accuracy.

The musical notes over the second stanza of the M425 Ode to Phyllis record the same melody that Guido wrote over Paul the Deacon's words. Each half-line or phrase starts one note higher in the hexachord than its predecessor. If the Ode is set at the same starting pitch, there is a perfect match between the tones at the start of each phrase and an almost precise match in all the notes that follow. There can be no doubt that the one melody is directly taken from the other. A complete interpretation of the M425 neumes of the Ode to Phyllis is given in Appendix II, together with a more developed, if more speculative, musical rendering on a treble stave. Here are the basic readings of the Guido and Horace melodies:

Guido:	**Horace:**
CDFDED	CDFDED
ut queant laxis	*multa qua crines*
DDCDEE	DDCDEE
resonare fibris	*religata fulges*
EEGEDECD	EGEDECD
mira gestorum	*ridet argento*
FGAGFEDD	FGAGFFD
famuli tuorum	*domus ara castis*

GAGFEFGD
solve polluti

GAGEFGGD
vincta verbenas

AGAFGAA
labii reatum

AGAFGAA
avet immolato

GFDCED
sancte Iohannes

GADCEED
spargier agno

The dating of the two documents makes clear that the tune in Guido's letter to Michael is taken from Horace's Ode to Phyllis melody, and not the other way round. Guido's written account also seems to suggest that the tune did not originate from any known setting of the *Hymn to St John the Baptist*, as Paul the Deacon's poem became known in the English-speaking world. Musically, as Appendix II suggests, the melody seems to belong to a secular song rather than a formal religious hymn. Indeed, there is internal evidence in the M425 music that confirms the Horatian melody was specifically composed for the Ode. In both the fifth and sixth stanzas, there are musical embellishments that seem clearly designed to bring out nuances in the text. The early part of the piece describes Horace's preparations for a party and comes to a climax when he reveals, in line two of the fifth stanza, that these are because it is Maecenas's birthday. The Latin *"quod"* for "because" is not sung purely on the note G, as are the matching words in the other stanzas, but on an FG quaver. And in line three of the next stanza, there is an unusual weak *caesura* when the final vowel of *"lasciva"* is attached to the first half-line. Here both the songwriter and the musical arranger play games with the tempo. *Lasciva"* means "sexy", a combination of wilfulness, playfulness and overt sexuality. The music seems to call for a rubato on the first two syllables, followed by a staccato final "-a" before the tune picks up again.

As the foremost music-teacher of his time, Guido must have known that the source of his ut-re-mi melody was Horace's Ode to Phyllis. The only text where this melody is known to exist in early medieval manuscripts is in M425. Guido could have read or heard the song in many places during his career. It is unlikely, however, that he saw the M425 codex at Pomposa, as in that case he would not have needed to write a letter to Michael about it. Furthermore, although the Pomposa library was reputed to be the largest in Italy outside Monte Cassino, no version of Horace's works was recorded in Abbot Geronimo's catalogue completed in 1093. It is sensible to conclude that Guido found the text, or another like it, in some unknown place on the travels he is thought to have made in northern Europe.

There is a possibility that Guido saw the M425 manuscript itself, because the music he used is a close match with the second stanza, and it could be significant that in this codex the second stanza is fully legible, while the first stanza is partly obscured. On the other hand, the very small differences in a few of the musical embellishments could suggest either subtle variations by Guido, or that he had come across a slightly different version of the Ode, which has now been lost.

There is a clue in the text of Paul the Deacon's poem that supports the case that Guido deliberately used it as an 'envelope' for the music from Horace's ode. As in several aspects of this mystery, the truth has been obscured because musicologists and musical historians generally know little about the lyric song of the Augustan age, and most classicists know little about medieval music. Conventionally, Paul's verses have been set out by music scholars in couplets, partly because the first four phrases appear to rhyme and partly because it seemed logical to highlight ut-re-mi-fa-sol-la at the beginning of each line. This misapprehension was aggravated by the fact that several works of reference present the first word of the sixth half-line as *'labi'*, even though *'labi'* would in this context mean the grammatically unnatural 'for a stain', the dative case of *'labes'*.

What Paul wrote was *'labii'*, the genitive case of *'labium'* ('of the lip'). This small correction makes a huge difference to the scansion. His thirteen stanza poem was in fact written not in couplets, but in Horatian Sapphics, his only surviving poem to use that metre. The Ode to Phyllis and the Hymn to St John have an identical metrical form. The syllables in the first three lines of each stanza are hendecasyllabic with, in sequence, long – long – short – long – long, a breathing space known as a *caesura*, and then short – short – long – short – long and a final syllable that can be either long or short. The fourth line has only five syllables, long – short – short – long and a fifth syllable that can be either long or short.

Horace's lines are:

> *multa, qua crines religata fulges;*
> *ridet argento domus; ara castis*
> *vincta verbenis avet immolato*
>   *spargier agno.*

Paul the Deacon wrote:

ut queant laxis resonare fibris
mira gestorum famuli tuorum,
solve polluti labii reatum,
  sancta Iohannes!

Nothing could have been simpler than to move the melody across from the Ode to Phyllis to the Hymn to John the Baptist. Sapphics to Sapphics, the rhythmic fit is perfect, providing an ideal vehicle for one of Guido's classroom exercises.

Why did Guido hide the fact that his music for ut-re-mi came from a Horatian song? It could have been simply that Horace's Latin did not suit his purpose in terms of euphony or general philosophy. A more profound answer may lie in the unpredictability of an age when unorthodox beliefs or the pressures of religious politics could put anyone's life at risk.

As a young boy at Pomposa, Guido will have been aware of the fate of Wilgard, a well-known grammarian in Ravenna, thirty miles away. Wilgard attempted to revive classical literature and declared there was as much truth in the Latin poets as in the revelations of the Holy Scriptures. He paid for his belief by being burned at the stake.

Wherever Guido came across Horace's Ode to Phyllis, he must have been concerned at its content. A lamb was to be sacrificed on a pagan altar. April is described as the month of Venus of the Sea. The final exhortation is from the songwriter to a musician and mistress:

> "Come to me now, my own last love, –
> No other girl will keep me warm, –
> Learn, learn the music! Come along,
> And with your lovely voice perform!
> Dark cares will become less with song."

(IV.11)

These were not sentiments with which Guido could associate. Although he shared Horace's love of music, he could not have been a more different character. Horace was short, plump and extroverted, an Epicurean woman-iser and a pagan entertainer. Guido was spare, ascetic and highly-strung, a Benedictine celibate and a cathedral choirmaster. Horace was worldly, a charmer, not without courage, and capable of a polite refusal even to his head of state. Guido was unworldly, deferential and fearful, bruised by the set-backs of his youth, and shaped by his religion and institutions:

Neque decedit aerata triremi et
post equitem sedet atra Cura.
Black Anxiety
sits on the trireme with the brazen prow
and behind the horseman as he rides away.

(III.1)

Europe was still emerging from the Dark Ages when Guido made his discovery. He had suffered an envious backlash once before and it had led to his banishment from the only home he had known since childhood. Now, he announced his discovery in a letter to his closest friend and associate at Pomposa: "To the most blessed and beloved Brother Michael, Guido, by many vicissitudes cast down and strengthened."

Cautious and circumspect, Guido d'Arezzo hid the source of his musical mnemonic even from his oldest friend. He dared not write what could be distorted and used against him. No matter that many of Horace's songs praised moderation and human values. The Ode to Phyllis was immoral and irreligious. Some of Horace's other songs were worse. They presented God the Father as a seducer of womankind, attributed the qualities of the Son of God to the Emperor, and ignored the Holy Spirit and the promise of redemption after death. They glorified drunkenness, promiscuity and paganism, and were sexually crude and explicit. The works of Horace were banned at the Abbey of Cluny in France and in Rome.

Guido ascribed his new discovery to the grace of God: "Our actions are good," he wrote, "only when we ascribe to the Creator all that we are able to accomplish." How could he at the same time acknowledge the debt he owed to a musical setting of Horace's Ode to Phyllis?

The answer is that he could not. To do so would risk destroying the work of a lifetime and ending his life as a condemned heretic.

Guido d'Arezzo extricated himself from the dilemma with subtlety. He maintained continuity with St John, the subject of his old musical game. He chose blameless words from a saintly Benedictine scholar of the past. He obscured the source of the music. He created the idea, managed the selection, and joined the two together. This was his triumph and his secret. The origin of do-re-mi remained shrouded in mystery for nearly a thousand years.

Life of Horace
Chronological Table

Date BC	Rome	Horace
65	Pompey conquers Syria Manlius consul	Born in Venusia
60	First Triumvirate formed: Pompey, Crassus, J Caesar. Metellus consul	
55	Caesar invades Britain	
53	Crassus defeated by Parthians	
50	Civil War between Pompey and Caesar	At school in Rome
48	Defeat of Pompey at Pharsalia	
44	Caesar assassinated	Studies in Athens
43	Octavius consul Second Triumvirate formed: Mark Antony, Octavian, Lepidus	Joins Brutus's army
42	Battle of Philippi	Ignominious defeat described in II.7
40	Peace of Brundisium brokered by Maecenas	Working as a Treasury clerk
39	Peace of Puteoli	
38	Octavian loses sea battle of Scyllaeum against Pompeius Sextus	Introduced to Maecenas
37		Journey to Brundisium
36	Octavian's naval disaster at Palinurus Octavian defeats Pompeius Sextus Lepidus exiled	Shipwrecked at Palinurus[1]
35		First Book of Satires Receives Sabine Farm
33	Octavian's second consulship	
32	Antony divorces Octavia and bequeathes Eastern territories to Cleopatra and her sons	

---

[1] Date and circumstances conjectural, see Chapter 1.

31	Octavian's third consulship Battle of Actium	
30	Deaths of Antony and Cleopatra	*Nunc est bibendum* (I.37) Second Book of Satires Publication of Epodes
29	Octavian's triple triumph	
28	Consecration of Temple of Apollo	Composes I.31
27	Act of Settlement Octavian is named Augustus	Begins Roman Odes
26	Aelius Gallus: Arabian campaign	Ode to Iccius (I.29)
24	Augustus returns from Spain	
23	Constitutional crisis Death of Murena Fall of Maecenas	First three Books of Odes published
20	Recovery of standards from Parthia	First Book of Epistles
19		Deaths of Virgil and Tibullus
18	Passing of Julian family laws	
17	Centennial Games	*Carmen Saeculare*
15	Tiberius and Drusus defeat German tribes	Composes IV.14
13	Tiberius consul	Fourth Book of Odes
12	Augustus becomes Pontifex Maximus Death of Agrippa	Second Book of Epistles
10		*Ars Poetica*
9	Death of Drusus	
8	Death of Maecenas	Death of Horace

42

Translator's Note

As increasing numbers of students take Classical Studies without a developed understanding of Latin, there is an obvious need for an English verse translation of Horace's Odes. The project is not without risk. Only verse can convey the momentum and musicality of the original, but no English translation can fully replicate the polish and compactness of Horace's Latin.

For the most part, I have used traditional English metrical and rhyming schemes. Sometimes, this has meant stretching the Latin, as in the First Spring Ode (I.4) which invited the metrical scheme of Gray's *Elegy,* and I.34 and IV.10 which have become sonnets. For a few of the heavier and more formal prayers (I.2, I.12 and *Carmen Saeculare*) I have used an anglicised version of Horace's Sapphics, and for the jolly song to Neobule (III.12) I have reflected the original *Ionic a minore* metre. Compromise is inevitable. Occasionally, I have had to make do with near rhyme in order to keep the sense of the Latin original.

Horace's stringed instruments are the *lyra, barbiton* and *cithara.* My use of lyre, lute and the anachronistic "guitar" is less precise, and I have some-times used the terms interchangeably to meet the requirements of English rhyme. Similarly "flute", convenient for rhyming in English, is not quite the same as the ancient *aulos* or *tibia.* All these instruments are described in Landels (see Bibliography).

Although I have omitted some proper names and place names, where they are not particularly significant, most of them remain and are explained in the Glossary. Often, they have as much significance as common nouns and carry with them the inheritance of myth or history.

Index of Odes

Book I

13. **To Lydia**
When you extol Telephus' charms
Cum tu Lydia, Telephi

14. **To the Ship of State**
O ship, once more will the fierce wave
O navis, referent in mare te novi

15. **The Prophecy of Nereus**
The herdsman with his Idean navy
Pastor cum traheret per freta navibus

16. **A Lover's Apology**
O fairer daughter than a mother fair
O matre pulchra filia pulchrior

17. **To Tyndaris**
Swift Faunus often changes his retreat
Velox amoenum saepe Lucretilem

18. **To Varus**
Before the sacred vine, my friend
Nullam, Vare, sacra vite prius severis arborem

19. **Glycera**
Mother of Cupids, Venus wild
Mater saeva Cupidinum

20. **To Maecenas**
You'll drink from just an ordinary mug
Vile potabis modicis Sabinum

21. **Hymn to Diana and Apollo**
Sing of Diana, sing, young girls
Dianam tenerae dicite virgines

22. **To Fuscus**
The man, whose life is blameless and who goes
Integer vitae scelerisque purus

23. **To Chloe**
You are avoiding me like a young deer
Vitas inuleo me similis, Chloe

24. **To Virgil**
Mourning so dear a person, who can have
Quis desiderio sit pudor aut modus

25. **To Lydia**
Now impudent youths seldom throw
Parcius iunctas quatiunt fenestras

26. **For Lamia**
I'm a friend of the Muses, so sadness and fear
Musis amicus tristitiam et metus

27. **The Drinking Party**
Goblets were made to further man's delight
Natis in usum laetitiae scyphis

28. **Archytas and the Sailor**
Archytas, you once measured sea and land
Te maris et terrae numeroque carentis harenae

29. **To Iccius**
Do you now covet the Arabs' blessed store
Icci, beatis nunc Arabum invides

30. **Prayer to Venus**
Venus, Queen of Cnidos, pray
O Venus, regina Cnidi Paphique

31. **Prayer to Apollo**
What is the bard's behest
Quid dedicatum poscit Apollinem

32. **To the Lyre**
We're called. If ever, sitting in the shade
Poscimur. si quid vacui sub umbra

33. **To Tibullus**
Don't grieve too much in memory
Albi, ne doleas plus nimio memor

34. **On the Divine**
I seldom took the gods too seriously
Parcus deorum cultor et infrequens

35. **To Fortune**
O divine goddess of fair Antium
O diva, gratum quae regis Antium

36. **To Numida**
With lyre and incense I'll fulfil my vow
Et ture et fidibus iuvat

37. **The Death of Cleopatra**
Now is the time to drink and beat
Nunc est bibendum, nunc pede libero

38. **To a Slave Boy**
I loathe all lavish Persian decoration
Persicos odi, puer, apparatus

Book II

1. **To Asinius Pollio**
   The civil strife that in the bygone days
   Motum ex Metello consule civicum
2. **To Sallustius Crispus**
   Sallustius Crispus, no colour imbues
   Nullus argento color est avaris
3. **To Dellius**
   Keep a cool head when things are hard
   Aequam memento rebus in arduis
4. **To Xanthias of Phocis**
   You love a slave girl. Do not be ashamed
   Ne sit ancillae tibi amor pudori
5. **To Lalage's Admirer**
   She cannot with submissive neck support
   Nondum subacta ferre iugum valet
6. **To Septimius**
   You hope to travel with me to Cadiz
   Septimi, Gadis aditure mecum
7. **To Pompeius Varus**
   Into the hour of death you often came
   O saepe mecum tempus in ultimum
8. **To Barine**
   If any punishment for broken faith
   Ulla si iuris tibi peierati
9. **To Valgius Rufus**
   No, not forever does the piercing rain
   Non simper imbres nubibus hispidos
10. **To Licinius**
    Your life would be in better shape
    Rectius vives, Licini, neque altum
11. **To Quinctius Hirpinus**
    What the warlike Cantabrians may conspire
    Quid bellicosus Cantaber et Scythes
12. **To Maecenas**
    The long and fierce Numantian war
    Nolis longa ferae bella Numantiae

Book III

5. **The Example of Regulus**
   When Jupiter is thundering in the sky
   Caelo tonantem credidimus Iovem
6. **Rome's Moral Decline**
   Roman, though guiltless, you must now atone
   Delicta maiorum immeritus lues
7. **To Asterie**
   Why do you weep? The fair west wind
   Quid fles, Asterie, quem tibi candidi
8. **To Maecenas**
   What am I doing, you ask
   Martiis caelebs quid agam Kalendis
9. **The Poet and Lydia**
   As long as I was your delight
   Donec gratus eram tibi
10. **To Lyce**
    If you drank from the furthest Tanais
    Extremum Tanain si biberes, Lyce
11. **To Mercury and the Lyre**
    Mercury, who once in Amphion found
    Mercuri – nam te docilis magistro
12. **To Neobule**
    It is not done for poor girls to play
    Miserarum est neque amori
13. **The Bandusian Spring**
    Spring of Bandusia more bright than glass
    O fons Bandusiae splendidior vitro
14. **To the Common People of Rome**
    Like Hercules, Augustus sought the rewards
    Herculis ritu modo dictus, o plebs
15. **To Chloris**
    You are just a poor man's wife
    Uxor pauperis Ibyci
16. **To Maecenas**
    For captive Danae a tower of bronze
    Inclusam Danaen turris aenea
17. **To Aelius Lamia**
    Aelius, after old Lamus nobly named
    Aeli vetusto nobilis ab Lamo

18. **Hymn to Faunus**
Faunus, the Nymphs flee at your love
Faune, Nympharum fugientum amator

19. **To Telephus**
How many years there are from Inachus
Quantum distet ab Inacho

20. **To Pyrrhus**
Don't you see that a lioness
Non vides quanto moveas periclo

21. **For Corvinus (To a Wine Jar)**
O sister, born in the same year as I
O nata mecum consule Manlio

22. **To Diana**
Guard of the mountains, Virgin of the grove
Montium custos nemorumque, Virgo

23. **To Phidyle**
If you have raised open hands to the sky
Caelo supinas si tuleris manus

24. **Rome's Immorality**
Though wealthier than the untapped stores
Intactis opulentior

25. **To Bacchus**
Where do you take me, as I rave
Quo me, Bacche, rapis tui

26. **Prayer to Venus**
Of girls till now I'd never tire
Vixi puellis nuper idoneus

27. **To Galatea**
The unholy should go on their way
Impios parrae recinentis omen

28. **To Lyde**
What better could I do on the holiday
Festo quid potius die

29. **To Maecenas**
Son of Etruscan kings of yore
Tyrrhena regum progenies

30. **Epilogue**
I've made a monument to outlast bronze
Exegi monumentum aere perennius

Book IV
1. **To Venus**
   Venus, are you resuming war
   Intermissa, Venus, diu
2. **To Iullus**
   Whoever, Iullus, strives to emulate
   Pindarum quisquis studet aemulari
3. **To Melpomene**
   He, whom at birth with kindly eye
   Quem tu Melpomene semel
4. **In Praise of Drusus**
   Like the winged servant of the thunderbolt
   Qualem ministrum fulminis alitem
5. **To Augustus Caesar**
   Born of the good gods, guardian excellent
   Divis orte bonis, optime Romulae
6. **Hymn to Apollo**
   O god, your vengeance at their massive boast
   Dive, quem proles Niobea magnae
7. **To Torquatus**
   The snows have scattered; now upon the leas
   Diffugere nives, redeunt iam gramina campis
8. **To Censorinus**
   I'd willingly give bowls and gifts of bronze
   Donarem pateras grataque commodus
9. **To Lollius**
   Lest you may think my words will die
   Ne forte credas interitura
10. **To Ligurinus**
    Still you are cruel, although the gifts of love
    O crudelis adhuc et Veneris muneribus potens
11. **To Phyllis**
    I've a full flask of Alban wine
    Est mihi nonum superantis annum
12. **To Virgil**
    Now spring's companions who calm the seas
    Iam veris comites, quae mare temperant

13. **To Lyce**
The gods have heard my prayers; you're getting old
Audivere, Lyce, di mea vota, di
14. **To Augustus Caesar**
How will the Senate and People of Rome
Quae cura patrum quaeve Quiritium
15. **The Augustan Age**
When Phoebus saw I wished to tell the tale
Phoebus volentem proelia me loqui

Carmen Saeculare: The Centennial Hymn
Phoebus and mighty Diana holding sway
Phoebe silvarumque potens Diana

Book I

I.1
To Maecenas

Maecenas born of ancient royal line,
Guardian, protector and sweet pride of mine,
Some men in racing chariots love to pound
The Olympic dust; their red-hot wheels scrape round
The marker posts; they win the noble palm,
And earthly lords then gods in heaven become.
One, if a mob of fickle burghers vies
To raise with triple honours, wins his prize;
One, if in his own granary is kept
All that from Libyan threshing-floors is swept.
A man, who glad at heart applies his hoe
To cleave his father's fields, would never go
To be a trembling mariner afloat
The sea of Myrtos in a Cyprian boat.
The merchant, when the wind from Africa raves
Locking in combat with the Icarian waves,
In trepidation lauds the life of leisure
He spends in his home town, and country pleasure;
But soon his battered ship is in repair,
For poverty he's not been taught to bear!
One man loves goblets of old Massic wine
And steals a long siesta, to recline
Stretched out beneath a green arbutus or
By a slow source of sacred water. More
Enjoy a military camp, the sound
Of trumpet mixed with cornet all around,
And warfare which their mother execrates.
The hunter under freezing heaven waits

Until, as he his soft young wife forgets,
A Marsian boar breaks through tight-woven nets
Or faithful hounds a fallow deer espy.
I am uplifted to the gods on high
By ivy garlands, prizes in the school,
Of learned poesy. The woodlands cool,
And Nymphs and Satyrs dancing with light grace,
Divide me from the ordinary race
Of men, if Muse Euterpe plays the flute
And Polyhymnia tunes the Lesbian lute;
But if you count me among the lyric bards,
My head will be so high, I'll hit the stars.

I.2
To Augustus Caesar

Our Father has sent down to earth enough snow
And terrible hail. He has hurled his bolts down
At Rome's holy places, his right hand aglow,
    And frightened the town,

Frightened the people that Pyrrha's grim time
Will return. In years past she bewailed portents strange:
Old Proteus drove herds from deep ocean to climb
    The high mountain range,

And fishes all clung to the tops of elm trees
Where turtledoves had their familiar abode,
And petrified deer swam in cascading seas.
    Yellow Tiber flowed

Just now, as we've seen, with its waves twisted back
In violent motion from the Etruscan shore
To throw royal monuments down in its track
    And to turn o'er

The Temple of Vesta. Yes, Tiber, who loves
Sad Ilia his consort, slips leftwards and swanks
He'll avenge her by straying (though Jove disapproves)
    Over his banks.

Youth's numbers are few, through the sins of the father;
They'll hear how our citizens sharpened the sword
That should have brought death to grim Parthians rather
    Than civil discord.

Which god should our people invoke to arrest a
Collapse of the Empire? With what hymn or prayer
Can our holy virgins wear down divine Vesta
    Unwilling to hear?

Which god will Jove order to expiate our crime?
We pray that with bright shoulders cloaked in a cloud
Prophetic Apollo will come in due time,
    Or laughing out loud

The goddess of Eryx, around whom cavort
Winged Cupid and Mirth, or our ancestor Mars
To his spurned race returned, fed up with the sport
    Of long drawn out wars,

The cry of the battlefield, helmets afire,
The keen visaged African foot soldier glaring
At a blood spattered foe; or you, son of dear Maia,
    Mercury, daring

To fly down and change your own form to the frame
Of a young man on earth and, braving the danger,
To suffer the people to give you the name
    Of Caesar's avenger.

Do not return heavenwards too soon! May you long
Be happy among us and, pray, do not seize
Unjustly upon every fault and each wrong!
    Nor may a breeze

Too swift snatch you up! Here great triumphs be yours!
May you love the names Father and Prince, and may you
Take your revenge on the Medes and their horse,
    Rome's Caesar new!

I.3
For Virgil

Venus over Cyprus reigning,
    Castor, Pollux, brightly shining,
Aeolus father of the winds
    Who his other children binds –
If he follows my behest –
    Save Iapyx in the west,
Heavenly gods, guide Virgil's ship
    Charged to bear him on this trip.

Good ship also, I implore,
    Bring him safe to Athens' shore,
Keep your promised cargo whole
    And save half of my own soul.
Oaken heart and brazen chest
    He who first put to the test
Fragile craft on cruel seas.
    He feared not the African breeze
Battling head-on with the blast
    Of northerlies approaching fast,
Hyades which ill presage,
    Or southerly with furious rage,
The Adriatic lord who'll tell
    If to raise or calm the swell.
Death's tread was not feared by him,
    Dry eyed he saw monsters swim,
Turbulent seas he saw and worse,
    Epirus' rocks, the sailor's curse.
God, pursuing a vain notion,
    Parts lands with estranging ocean,
But heretical craft still please
    To leap across untouchable seas.
Boldly exploring, mankind's throng
    Dives into forbidden wrong.
Bold Prometheus by a fraud
    Brought men fire, an ill reward;
Filched from its ethereal home,
    Fire made cruel consumption come:
A novel host of fevers then
    Settled on the lands of men
And the necessity, once late,
    Of distant death picked up its gait.

Daedalus tried the empty air
　　On wings not given man to share;
Hercules broke through Acheron.
　　Naught by mortals can't be done.
We in our stupidity
　　Try to reach the very sky,
Not allowing through our faults
　　God to still his thunderbolts.

I.4
To Sestius

Keen winter melts, the pleasant time of spring
　　Has come in its due turn, the west wind blows,
And from the shipyards engines start to bring
　　The dry hulls down to where the water flows.

The herd no longer joys in stables warm,
　　Nor ploughman in the hot fire's glowing light;
The hoar-frost settles not upon the farm,
　　And pastures green no longer turn to white.

Now Cytherean Venus leads the dance,
　　The ascending moon illuminates the sky,
And comely Graces with the Nymphs advance,
　　Joined hand in hand in perfect modesty.

With left foot, then with right, alternately,
　　They shake the earth in rhythm to their hymn,
While ardent Vulcan leaves his home to see
　　The Cyclopes at work in factories grim.

Now is the time to crown your shining head
    With heavy leaves from the green myrtle tree
Or with fresh flowers taken from their bed,
    The flowers that the loosened soils set free.

Now also is the time to sacrifice
    In woods that from the sun lie darkly hid
To Faunus, known as Pan, his stated price,
    A lamb or, if he should prefer, a kid.

Pale death with undiscriminating tread
    Knocks at kings' castles and the poor man's inn,
And life's brief sum, o blessed friend soon dead,
    Does not allow us long hopes to begin.

The pressing night will soon upon you come,
    The shades and ghosts that storytellers know,
And cheerless Pluto's unsubstantial home;
    And once you thither on your journey go

You'll not be chosen King of Wine by lot,
    Nor stop and stare at Lycidas's charm;
Now he makes all the young men boiling hot,
    And soon the young ladies will grow quite warm!

I.5
To Pyrrha

Who's the slim boy pressing on you
　　Among the rose petals, Pyrrha,
Soaked with perfumes his body through
　　In a secluded cave somewhere?

Now you tie back your flaxen hair,
　　Simple and neat beneath his gaze;
Ah, but in tears he soon will swear
　　Faith and the gods have changed their ways.

He will stare out and watch the sea
　　Boil at black winds. How raw he is,
Who now enjoys you credulously,
　　Hoping your golden self is his,

Free to be loved, single, untied
　　Always; not knowing the false breeze!
I pity those who have not tried
　　Your shining waters. Through with the seas,

My plaque on Neptune's temple wall
　　Shows that in dedication I
Have hung my sodden garments all
　　In honour of his potency!

I.6
To Agrippa

Your bravery and victories o'er the foe
    Let Varius, our Homeric songbird, pen! –
Ferocious feats that all the world should know,
    Performed on ship and horse by Agrippa's men.

These noble themes I'll not attempt to write,
    Nor wily Odysseus' course across the sea,
Dauntless Achilles' stomach for the fight,
    And Pelops' house with its foul savagery.

Too slight for such grand things, my sense of shame
    And Muse that governs an unwarlike lyre
Bar me from spoiling excellent Caesar's name
    And yours with praise my talents can't inspire.

Of Meriones black with Trojan dust,
    Or adamantine Mars dressed for the fight,
Or godlike Diomede, Minerva's trust,
    Some poets perhaps could with distinction write.

I sing of parties, of young girls who yearn
    To fight their boyfriends with trimmed fingernails.
I can be empty-headed or can burn –
    Whatever! My wit usually never fails!

I.7

To Plancus

Others can praise bright Rhodes or Mytilene
  Or Ephesus or Corinth's walls between
Two seas, Thebes (Dionysus' noted city),
  Apollo's Delphi, Thessaly's Tempe pretty;
And some sing endless songs to add renown –
  Their life's sole work – to Virgin Pallas' town,
Tearing down olive leaves to bind their brow.
  Many, to honour Juno, will avow
That Argos with its horses is divine
  Or sumptuous Mycenae is more fine.
Enduring Sparta and the open plain
  Of fertile Larissa, these yet again
Have never struck me so much as the home
  Of resonant Albunea or the foam
Of hurtling Anio or Tibur's lush wood
  And orchards where the mobile rivulets flood.
Clear south winds often wipe clouds from dark skies
  And showers don't last forever. If you're wise,
Remember to end your sadness; with sweet wine
  Soften life's labours, whether standards shine
Around you in the barracks or you're laid
  Resting beneath your own Tibur's thick shade.
Teucer escaping Salamis, it's said,
  And fleeing from his father, his forehead
Damp from Bacchus, around his temples tied
  A poplar crown. To his sad friends he cried:
"Wherever fortune takes us, it will prove
  Better, my comrades, than a father's love.

Abandon not your hope while Teucer is
  Your leader and observes the auspices.
Unerring Phoebus promised there would stand
  A second Salamis in a new land.
O brave companions, you have often dared
  Worse things with me and my misfortunes shared.
Now turn to wine and drive away your sorrow;
  We'll sail the vast sea once more on the morrow!"

I.8
To Lydia

Lydia, please tell me this
  Truly, by the gods above!
Why do you drive Sybaris
  To distraction with your love?

Now he hates the field of sports,
  Though he once bore dust and sun,
Refuses to ride a horse
  With an armed companion,

Will not break a Gallic mare
  Straining at a sharp-toothed curb,
Yellow Tiber doesn't dare
  Touch. Now, wrestling oils disturb

Him more than a viper's blood.
  His arms are no longer blue,
Bruised from weapons. Often he would
  Win first prize at discus throw,

And the javelin he would fling
  Far beyond the boundary line.
Why is he hiding, as – poets sing –
  Once the son of the Marine

Thetis at Troy's tearful end
  Hid, in case his manly dress
Should before his due time send
  Him to the Lycian ranks and death?

I.9
To the Master of Wine

Soracte stands before your eyes
    White with deep snow, the labouring woods
    Can't hold their burden, and the floods
Are stilled, set fast with jagged ice.

So come and melt away the cold,
    Pile the logs high upon the fire,
    And generously from a Sabine jar
Draw off a vintage four years old.

The rest leave to the gods! They make
    The winds that battle on raging sea
    At once grow calm, and instantly
Cypress and old ash cease to shake.

Don't ask what will tomorrow bring!
    Count every day, that Chance above
    Shall grant, a plus! Shun not sweet love
Or, while you're young, to dance and sing!

For now you are green, and grey hair sour
    Is far off. Sports field and the square,
    Smooth whispers in the twilight air
Must be claimed now at the appointed hour, –

Soft laughter that betrays a girl
    Who in some deep nook hides her charms,
    And a pledge stolen from her arms
Or finger that will just uncurl!

I.10
Hymn to Mercury

O Atlas' grandson, smooth and eloquent,
    Primitive men were savage and unkempt!
You moulded us with language and the rule,
    Shrewd Mercury, of the decorous wrestling school.

O messenger of gods and Jove their king,
    O father of the curved lyre, I'll sing
Of you and your skill, when you hide away
    Whatever you desire in furtive play.

When you removed his oxen by your craft,
    Apollo, empty quivered, stood and laughed.
He scared you, still a child, with menacing cries,
    If you did not give back the stolen prize.

Rich Priam escaped the Atrides in their pride,
    When he left Ilium with you as guide;
He slipped past the watch fires of Thessaly
    And the encampment of Troy's enemy.

You lay the spirits of the good to rest
    Within the settled realms of happiness;
Your gold wand rules the unsubstantial host,
    Friend of the highest gods and nethermost.

I.11

To Leuconoe
"Carpe diem"

Ask not what term the gods have granted me
    Or granted you! To know is surely wrong.
Ignore the numbers of astrology
    And do not test the charts of Babylon!

It's better far to suffer what will be,
    Whether God has allotted winters more,
Or this your last wears out the Etruscan Sea
    Upon the pumice rocks that guard the shore.

Be smart, my dear! Filter the wine instead!
    Cut back long hope to the brief space you borrow!
While we talk, envious lifetime will have fled.
    Harvest the day, and do not trust tomorrow!

I.12

Prayer for Augustus Caesar

What man or which hero deserving of fame
To the sound of the lyre or shrill pipe will you sing,
O Clio? Which god? And which is the name
    Whose echo will ring

In jest on the shady sides of Helicon
Or on Pindar's summit or Haemus' mount chill,
Where thoughtless woods followed Orpheus and the song
    He chanted to still

The fast falling rivers and swift rushing winds
With his mother's spell, the Muse Calliope,
As he charmed the attentive oak trees with his strings
    That sang so sweetly?

But first, with the praise that our custom demands,
I'll tell of our Father who guides with his powers
Men's and gods' affairs, and the world, sea and lands
    With their changing hours.

From him is begotten no one to compare,
Not like him or second or that can surpass,
Though next to him honours are taken by fair
    Athenian Pallas.

Nor will I ignore you, so bold in the fight,
O Liber, and Virgin Diana the foe
Of wild beasts; or, feared for your arrow's sure flight,
    Phoebus Apollo.

I'll tell, too, of Hercules and Leda's sons,
One peerless at boxing, one matchless on horse:
As soon as seafarers spy that refulgence
    From their pure white stars,

Then down from the rocks the tossed waters soon flow,
The winds fall in concert and all the clouds flee,
The menacing wave – once they've wished it so –
    Subsides in the sea.

I could after these first of Romulus sing,
Pompilius' quiet reign, Tarquin's rod and his pride,

Or I might perhaps with stout Cato begin, –
   How nobly he died!

Regulus, the Scauri and Paulus' abuse
Of his mighty soul when Carthage vanquished us
I'll gladly recall with Rome's glorious Muse,
   Or Fabricius.

So, too, Curius with his dishevelled head
And Camillus likewise were made fit for war
By harsh poverty, an ancestral homestead
   And a suitable Lar.

Like a tree of unknown age, Marcellus's fame
Keeps growing, and high among all earthly stars,
The Julian star, like a great moon aflame,
   Gleams mid lesser fires.

O Father and Guardian of the human race,
Begotten of Saturn, the Fates bid you care
For Caesar. May you reign and, in second place,
   Augustus Caesar!

Whether he drives off the Parthian hordes,
Their threat against Rome with just triumph subdued,
Or conquers the Chinese on far eastern shores
   And Indians rude,

Beneath you with justice he'll rule a glad world,
And you'll shake Olympus with your awesome car.
Upon unholy groves you'll fling thunderbolts, hurled
   In wrath from afar.

I.13
To Lydia

When you extol Telephus' charms,
  His rosy neck, his waxen arms,
I become bilious – ah, well! –
  My liver starts to seethe and swell.

My mind and colour don't stay still
  And furtively a tear will spill
Onto my cheeks and clearly show
  How my heart wastes with fires slow.

I burn when quarrels fuelled by wine
  Have spoiled your shoulders white and fine
Or if in wild passion the youth
  Has branded your lip with his tooth.

No, if you truly heeded me,
  You would not hope he'd constant be
Who loves to savage the sweet lips
  That Venus in her nectar dips.

Thrice happy those and more than thrice
  Whom an unbroken love knot ties;
No harsh word will their true love fray
  Until they reach their dying day.

I.14
To the Ship of State

O ship, once more will the fierce wave
Take you to sea? Ah, what's to do?
Hold fast to harbour and be brave!
Your side is bare of oars: don't you
    See this, and how the African blast
    Has left you with a wounded mast?

Your yardarms groan. Without a cable
Your hull can hardly against a swell
Of such imperiousness keep stable.
Intact you've not a single sail,
    Nor have you gods with whom to plead
    In this your second time of need.

You may be pine from Black Sea coasts,
A noble daughter of the seas;
Lineage and line are idle boasts.
The fearful sailor on the seas
    Trusts not in painted poops. Take stock,
    Unless you want the winds to mock!

Of late you were my deep concern,
My wearisome anxiety;
Now for your safety I still yearn,
And this is no slight care for me.
    Avoid the currents of the seas
    Around the shining Cyclades!

I.15
The Prophecy of Nereus

The herdsman with his Idean navy
Passed through the straits and, treacherous, dragged away
His hostess Helen. Then wise Nereus cast
Unwelcome sleep upon the tailwinds fast,
That he might sing the savage fates to come:
"With evil auguries you take her home,
Whom Greece with many a soldier will recover;
For Greece will swear an oath to tear your lover
And you apart, and Priam's kingdom old.
Woe to the horses and the warriors bold!
How great the sweat! What piles of death you amass
For Dardanus's race! Even now, Pallas
Prepares her helmet and her bronze attire,
Her chariots and her consuming ire.
Vainly, with arrogant trust that Venus may
Protect you, you will comb your hair and play
Songs women love to hear on the unwarlike lyre,
And vainly to your bedroom you'll retire,
Avoiding deadly spears, barbed darts from Crete,
The din of battle, Ajax' swift pursuit.
But in the end, alas, you surely must
Defile well-groomed adultery with dust.
Laertes' son who marks your people's end,
And Nestor whom the folk of Pylos send,
See you not them? Teucer from Salamis
And Sthenelus, who in close combat is
A champion and no idle charioteer
When horses need firm governance, press on near
Undaunted. You will recognise Merion.

See! See how in black fury Tydeus' son,
His father's better, seeks you out, while you, –
Just as a deer, when a wolf comes into view
Across the valley, will its grass forget, –
You'll run, with high-pitched breaths, effeminate.
This was not what you promised to your love!
Achilles' wrathful fleet will yet put off
The day for Phrygian mothers and for Troy:
Their ordained sum of winters they'll enjoy;
But, after that, Achaean flames will come
And burn the homes of Trojan Ilium."

I.16
A Lover's Apology

O fairer daughter than a mother fair,
    Impose whatever sentence you decree
On my slanderous iambics, whether you care
    To burn them or to throw them in the sea.

Not Dindymene, nor Apollo divine,
    The Pythian god and dweller of Delphi,
So shake the minds of their priests in their shrine,
    Nor Liber; nor the monks of Cybele

So clash their shrill cymbals, as anger sad
    That fears not Serbian sword, nor the event
Of shipwreck at sea, nor infernos mad,
    Nor Jupiter's tumultuous descent.

Prometheus added to the primal slurry
    Under compulsion, so it's said, a part
Extracted from each creature, and the fury
    Of the insane lion was grafted on our heart.

Anger brought Thyestes ruinously low
    And was the final cause for cities tall
To perish utterly, and the haughty foe
    Turned over with his plough the impressed wall.

Compose yourself! The passion in my breast, –
    For I was angry, too, and young and sweet, –
My raging passion put me to the test
    And made me pen those swift iambic feet

In fury. Now I want sadness to end
    And change to gentleness. Oh, now you see
My cruel taunts' recantation, be my friend:
    Give back your heart and give mine back to me!

I.17
To Tyndaris

Swift Faunus often changes his retreat
    On Mount Lycaeus for this lovely hill,
Defending my goats from the fiery heat
    Of summer, and from winds and rainstorms chill.

The nannies roam safely across the estate
To see where wild thyme and the arbutus hide,
Those wandering wives of a foul-smelling mate!
They're not afraid of the green serpents' bite

Nor of the martial wolves stalking on high,
Whenever with the sweet pipes' tune, my friend,
The valleys and the polished rocks that lie
In gentle Ustica echo to their end.

The gods protect me and the gods hold dear
My piety and my Muse. For you there'll be
An overflowing cornucopia here
Of glorious rural hospitality.

Here you'll escape in my secluded vale
The dog days' heat. The Teian lyre you'll play
And tell of two loves sighing for one male,
Penelope, and Circe bright as day.

Here, in the shade, you'll rest awhile and pour
Deep goblets of my harmless Lesbian wines.
No Mars or drunken Bacchus will make war.
You won't be afraid of Cyrus's designs –

That impudently he may come and dare
Throw bold hands on your barely matched weakness,
And tear apart the garland in your hair
And innocently undeserving dress.

I.18
To Varus

Before the sacred vine, my friend,
    Don't plant a single tree
In the soft soil of Tibur and
    Around Catilus' wall!
For truly what God sets before
    Teetotallers is all
Rough fare, and only wine makes
    Mordant worries flee.

After wine, who bleats of grim
    Service or poverty?
Who would not rather toast the gods
    Of drinking and true loves?
But no one must transgress the bounds
    Modest Liber approves;
The Centaurs' and the Lapiths' deadly
    Fight over wine must be

A warning, and harsh Euhius
    Who afflicts the Thracians, too,
When they distinguish right from wrong
    With a too narrow line,
Greedy for gratification.
    But you, fair God of Wine,
I'll not unwanted wake you,
    Revealing to full view

The mysteries of your varied leaves.
  Calm the wild drum's excess
And Berecyntian horn, for blind
  Self-love attends close by,
And Boastfulness that lifts his empty
  Head far, far too high,
And, free with secrets, Trustfulness
  More transparent than glass!

I.19
Glycera

Mother of Cupids, Venus wild,
  Bacchus, Theban Semele's child,
Frolicsome Licentiousness,
  All put me under duress
To give back my heart and mind
  To the love I once resigned.

I'm on fire with passion for
  Glycera, whose skin glows so pure
Parian marble can't impress
  More than her own loveliness.
I burn at her wanton grace
  And her too seductive face.

Venus overwhelms me, quitting
    Cyprus, not a word permitting
Of the Scythians from the Black
    Sea or Parthian on horseback
Turned in spirited defence, –
    Nothing without relevance!

Bring me fresh turf here, young men!
    Bring me bunches of vervain!
Incense! And some bowls to hold
    Unmixed wine that's two years old!
Once a victim has been slain,
    Love will come in gentler vein.

I.20
To Maecenas

You'll drink from just an ordinary mug
    A common Sabine wine
That I once stored and sealed in a Greek jug,
    Distinguished knight of mine,

When in the theatre you drew such applause
    Ancestral Tiber's banks
And jesting Vatican's mount sent echoing roars
    And so returned their thanks.

Grapes tamed by Calenian press or Caecuban wines,
    Imbibe them if you will!
My cups aren't blended with Falernian vines
    Or those from a Formian hill.

I.21
Hymn to Diana and Apollo

Sing of Diana, sing, young girls!
    Sing, boys, of Cynthius with long curls
And Lato whom our supreme Jove
    Adores with deep, enduring love!

Praise her who joys in streams and woods
    Where leaves o'erhang the icy floods
Of Algidus, the dark forest scene
    Of Erymanth or Cragos green!

Young men, laud Tempe with like praise
    And Delos, Apollo's birthplace,
His quiver on his shoulder brave
    And lyre that once his brother gave!

War's tears, famine and pestilence
    He'll drive from Rome's people and Prince,
And send them to the Persian race
    And Britons, inspired by your prayers.

I.22

To Fuscus

The man, whose life is blameless and who goes
    Pure of wrongdoing, needs no Moorish spear,
Nor bow, nor quiver pregnant with arrows
    That on their tips a venomous poison bear,

Whether he makes his journey across the sands
    Of seething Syrtes or the inhospitable
Mountains of Caucasus or those far lands
    Washed by the Hydaspes renowned in fable.

A wolf came on me in a Sabine wood
    While I was singing of my Lalage,
Roaming outside my estate in carefree mood,
    And though I was unarmed, it fled from me, –

A monster such as Daunia could not rear,
    That warrior province with oak forests wide,
Nor Juba's land produce, Numidia,
    The parched wet nurse of many a lions' pride.

Set me upon the plains of sluggishness
    Where summer's breeze refreshes not one tree,
Upon the world's edge where dank mists oppress
    And Jupiter in his malignancy!

Set me beneath the chariot of the sun
    That comes too close, in lands that homes deny!
Sweet-laughing Lalage, she'll be the one
    I'll love; I'll love sweet-speaking Lalage.

I.23
To Chloe

You are avoiding me like a young deer
    Who seeks across the mountainside untrod
Her anxious mother, and with needless fear
    Is startled by the breezes and the wood.

Whether the supple leaves, when spring has come,
    Begin to bristle, or green lizards part
The blackberry bushes' brambles in autumn,
    She trembles, shaking in her knees and heart.

But I don't stalk you like a tiger wild
    Or lion of Gaetulia with a plan
To tear you in two. It's simply time, my child
    To leave your mother and follow a man.

I.24
To Virgil

Mourning so dear a person, who can have
    Proper restraint? Teach us, Melpomene,
    Your mournful songs with the voice clear and high
That with the stringed guitar your father gave!

So now perpetual sleep presses upon
    Quintilius. Restraint, untarnished Faith –
    The sister of Justice – and naked Truth,
When will they find the like of such a one?

On his death, Virgil, many good men have wept;
　　None has wept more than you. Pious in vain,
　　You beg the gods to bring him back again.
'Twas not for this that they his credit kept.

Though more seductively you ruled the lyre
　　Than Orpheus, and trees listened as you played,
　　Would blood return into an empty shade,
Which Mercury had once with rod so dire,

And deaf to prayers that seek the fates to bend,
　　Compelled to join the dark flock of the night?
　　'Tis hard, but patience makes the pain more light
Of that which it is sinful to amend.

I.25
To Lydia

Now impudent youths seldom throw
　　Their volleys at your closed window.
They don't deprive you of your sleep,
　　But door is in love with doorstep,

When once it slid on an easy hinge.
　　Now, less and less, you hear them whinge,
"I'm yours and through the long nights die,
　　And, Lydia, do you sleeping lie?"

Instead, you'll weep, a poor old maid,
    At fornicators who've betrayed
You, slighted in a lonely alley
    As winds from Thrace make Bacchic sally

When the old moon gives way to new.
    Then, blazing love, wild passion, too,
That drives mares crazy, will engage
    And round your ulcerous liver rage.

And you'll complain that cheerful boys
    Rather in green ivy rejoice
And dark myrtle, and dedicate
    Dry leaves to Hebrus, winter's mate.

I.26
For Lamia

I'm a friend of the Muses, so sadness and fear
    I'll consign to the violent winds to bear
To the Cretan Sea, and I simply don't care
    Which king underneath the Northern Star
Creates some panic on a frozen shore,
    Or why Tiridates is struck by terror.

Sweet Muse, who in pure flowing springs has such fun,
    Weave garlands of flowers that bloom in the sun,
And weave my dear Lamia a musical crown!
    Without you, sweet Pimplean Muse, the renown
I confer profits nothing, so let honours come
    With new-fangled strings and a Lesbian plectrum!
May you and your sisters be pleased to consent
    To Lamia being honoured with your sacrament.

I.27
The Drinking Party

"Goblets were made to further man's delight;
    It's just the Thracians who use them to fight.
So give up these barbaric ways of yours!
    Keep modest Bacchus out of bloody brawls!

Lamplight and wine, and a Mede's scimitar,
    Are poles apart. What godless souls you are!
Control your shouting! Voices down, my friends!
    Keep to your seats, and please control your hands!"

"Must I drink rough Falernian wine as well?"
    "Megilla's brother from Opus must tell
What is this wound that he's so pleased to cherish,
    Whose arrow is it causes him to perish."

"You're not keen? I'll drink for no other price.
    Your amorous transgressions are so nice
And well bred! By whatever love you're tamed,
    You burn with fires that can't make you ashamed!

Whatever you may say, our ears are sure
    Repositories." "Oh, dear! What a whore!
A whirlpool. What a workload! What a dame!
    Poor boy, you do deserve a better flame.

What sorceress with drugs from Thessaly
    Can free you? What wizard? What god on high?
Even Pegasus could barely extricate
    You, caught up in Chimaera's triple shape!"

I.28
Archytas and the Sailor

"Archytas, you once measured sea and land
    And the numberless sand;
Now by the Matine shore your slight reward must
    Be a handful of dust
Confining you. To you no good has come
    From exploring heaven's home
Or running o'er the round arch of the sky
    With a mind doomed to die.

Pelops' father died, and with gods he dined!
　　And to the gentle wind
Tithonus was removed, and Minos too,
　　Who God's own secrets knew.
Panthoides the depths of Tartarus hold,
　　Twice down to Orcus called;
He, invoking the Trojan age, revealed
　　By taking down his shield
That nothing save his sinews and his skin
　　To dark death had he given,
No mean authority of nature, in your view,
　　And of that which is true.
But one night waits for all men, and death's road
　　Must once by all be trod.
The Furies present some men in a show
　　For grim Mars. Sailors go
To meet their end in grasping ocean's waves.
　　　　And so the mingled graves
Of old men and of young are quickly piled.
No head is spared by Proserpina wild."

"I, too, was taken when the swift south wind,
　　Sloping Orion's friend,
O'erwhelmed me in waves of the Illyrian Sea.
　　Do not be niggardly
Or grudge a particle of shifting sand
　　For my bones, sailor, and
Unburied head! So, when the east wind raves
　　Against the western waves,
Venusian woods be punished, you be spared!
　　And may a rich reward,

From every source it can, to you flow down,
   From Jupiter and Neptune
In whose care sacred Tarentum belongs!
   Will you commit such wrongs
As harm your innocent children after you?
   Perhaps the justice due
And lofty recompense may be your gift.
   No, I will not be left
With my prayers unavenged. No remedy
   Will ever set you free.
Although you hasten, it's no long delay:
Just throw dust down three times, then swift away!"

I.29
To Iccius

Do you now covet the Arabs' blessed store
   Of treasures, and prepare violent campaigns
Against the Sheban kings who ne'er before
   Were vanquished, and fashion your woven chains

For the rough Mede? Which of those foreign girls
   Will serve you when her young love has been slain?
Which princely boy with oiled and perfumed curls
   Will be assigned to fill your cup again,

Though he was taught to use his father's bow
   And fire oriental arrows? Who would deny
That rushing torrents can reverse their flow
   On sheer mountains, and Tiber backward fly,

When, in exchange for all the books you amass
   Of great Panaetius and the Academy,
You plan to purchase a Spanish cuirass,
   Though you once promised better things to me?

I.30
Prayer to Venus

Venus, Queen of Cnidos, pray,
Queen of Paphos, come away!
Your beloved Cyprus spurn!
Can't you smell the incense burn?
Glycera bids you fly across
And visit her lovely house.
Let your hot boy Cupid come,
Graces with girdles undone,
Hastening Nymphs, and Youth that is
Cruel without you, and Hermes!

I.31
Prayer to Apollo

What is the bard's behest
   At Apollo's consecration?
   As he pours his new libation,
What is the bard's request?

Not fertile acres of wheat
　　From Sardinia's rich soil!
　　Not the fine beasts of toil
Reared in Calabria's heat!

Not Indian ivory
　　Or gold! Not the countryside
　　Gnawed by the peaceful tide
Of mute Liris gliding by!

Let those, who such fortune share,
　　Prune the Calenian vine;
　　Let the rich merchant drink the wine
Bartered with Syrian ware,

And golden cups let him drain, –
　　To the very gods he is dear, –
　　For three or four times each year
He sails the Atlantic main

And survives! My favourite food
　　Is the fruit of the olive tree,
　　The endive or chicory,
And mallows light and good.

Grant, o Latona's son,
　　That in sound health and, I pray,
　　With an unimpaired mind I may
Enjoy the things I've won,

And grant that I do not mar
 Old age with dishonour, I pray,
 And let me continue to play
On the strings of my guitar.

I.32
To the Lyre

We're called. If ever, sitting in the shade,
 I've strummed a tune with you that, both this year
And in the years to come, will still be played,
 Come, sing a Latin song, o Grecian lyre!

First by a Lesbian citizen you were tuned,
 Who fought ferociously in time of war,
But in the lull of arms or having bound
 His storm tossed vessel on the wet seashore,

Of Liber and the Muses he would sing,
 Of Venus and the small boy at her side
Who to his mother constantly would cling,
 And handsome Lycus, black-haired and black-eyed.

O Phoebus' ornament, which Jove on high
 Welcomes at his banquets! Fair tortoiseshell!
Solace of labours and sweet remedy!
 Whenever I invoke you, treat me well.

I.33
To Tibullus

Don't grieve too much in memory
Of Glycera's cruel savagery
Or pitiful couplets rehearse,
Singing your elegiac verse,
Of why faith has been broken and
You're outshone by a younger man.
Lycoris, with her narrow brow,
Is passionate for Cyrus now,
But Cyrus turns his thoughts away
Towards abrasive Pholoe,
And yet a wild goat sooner might
With an Apulian wolf unite
Than Pholoe would sin and be
Found in base adultery.
This is one of Venus' designs,
Who, taking unlike forms and minds,
Sends them beneath her brazen yoke
As part of a barbaric joke.
Although I was loved by a better,
Myrtale bound me with a fetter,
Agreeable to me indeed,
But she's a slave who has been freed,
Fiercer than Adriatic waves
That bend the curved Calabrian bays.

I.34
On the Divine

I seldom took the gods too seriously.
I practised senseless wisdom and I strayed.
Now, I must set sail back again and try
Retrace the abandoned journeys I once made.
Jove, who with flashing fire oft parts the clouds,
Through a clear sky his thundering steeds has taken
And winged car, at which the wandering floods
And ponderous earth and River Styx are shaken,
And hateful Hell's cruel halls and Atlas' bounds.
God has the power to change lowest for high;
The great man of distinction he confounds;
He gives bright prominence to obscurity.
    From one man whistling Fortune steals the crest
    And laughs when by another it's possessed.

I.35
To Fortune

O divine goddess of fair Antium,
    Yours is the power to raise our mortal bones
From off the stepladder's most humble rung
    Or turn proud triumphs into grim tombstones.

You are solicited in anxious prayer
    By the poor tiller of the countryside
And, mistress of the deep, by whosoe'er
    Stirs with Bithynian keel the Carpathian tide.

The rough Dacian, the Scythian who flees,
    Cities and peoples and fierce Latium,
Mothers of kings in foreign monarchies
    And crimsoned tyrants fear that you will come

And with the foot of lawlessness kick down
    The standing column, and the throng will bray,
Inciting all the laggards of the town
    "To arms! To arms!" and shatter empire's sway.

Your slave Necessity strides on before,
    Waving her weapons, roof-beam fastenings,
And wedges brandished in her brazen claw;
    A dreadful hook and molten lead she brings.

Rare Faith, veiled in plain raiment of pure white,
    And Hope attend, and still as comrades come
Whenever you change clothes and in your spite
    Choose to abandon a once powerful home.

But then, the faithless mob and perjured whore
    Draw back, and when the wine jars are drained dry
Down to the dregs, false friends visit no more,
    Too treacherous to share adversity.

Save Caesar, who to the world's end departs
    Against the Britons! Save our hive's new swarm
Of young men to be feared in eastern parts
    And all around the Red Sea's waters warm.

Shame on our scars, our crimes, our brothers slain!
    Alas, our generation's hardened band

Held back from nothing. We have left a stain
　　Of universal wickedness. Youth's hand

Has stopped at naught in fear of gods on high,
　　Has spared no altar. Fortune, would you could
Against the Arabs and Massagetae
　　　　Reforge on anvils new our blunted sword!

I.36
To Numida

With lyre and incense I'll fulfil my vow
　　And with a calf's blood gladly will appease
The guardian gods of Numida, who now
　　Returns home safe from the far western seas.

To his dear friends he shares out many a kiss,
　　But none has more than Lamia sublime
Who was his king in boyhood's busy bliss
　　And donned a man's toga at the same time.

Let's mark with Cretan chalk this beautiful day
　　And let there be no limit to the wine
From an open jar, and in the Salian way
　　Let's give our feet no rest from dance divine!

Now Damalis likes her wine in unmixed doses,
　　But must not with one gulp drink Bassus silly.
No, at our feast let's have a mass of roses,
　　Long lasting celery and short-lived lily!

They'll all fix watery eyes on Damalis,
   But Damalis has a new paramour;
She won't be torn from that embrace of his.
   Indeed, the wanton ivy clings not more!

I.37
The Death of Cleopatra

Now is the time to drink and beat
   The ground with free and easy feet
And deck the cushions of the gods
   With sumptuously presented foods.

It would have been a sin before
   To bring wine from the ancestral store,
When Cleopatra's plans were all
   Mad ruin for the Capitol.

Death to the Empire she planned then
   With her diseased flock of foul men.
Wildly she hoped for each desire,
   Drunk with good fortune's sweet liqueur.

But then, her rage far less became,
   When from the burning fires there came
Scarcely one solitary ship
   Delivered safely from its trip.

She flew to Italy, her mind
    Distracted with Egyptian wine,
But Caesar pressing with his oars
    Soon drove her back to true terrors,

As though he were a hawk and she
    A gentle dove, or hunter he
Swiftly on Thessaly's snowy plains
    Chasing a hare, to put in chains

Fate's monster. She in nobler mood
    Sought her end, nor, as women could,
Shrank from the sword, nor did she race
    With her fleet to some hiding-place.

She dared with face serene to see
    Her fallen palace; then bravely
Fondled her deadly snakes until
    Her body drank the poison vile.

More fierce when she resolved to die,
    Scorning a jailer's cruel galley,
No humble woman, she ne'er sank
    To grace a proud triumph, stripped of rank.

I.38
To a Slave Boy

I loathe all lavish Persian decoration,
  Dislike crowns that with linden bark are bound;
My boy, don't bother seeking the location
  Where the late lingering rose is to be found!

I beg you, please, add no elaboration
  To simple myrtle. For you, serving the wine,
Myrtle is no indecent decoration,
  Or for me drinking under the thick vine.

Book II

II.1
To Pollio

The civil strife that in the bygone days
    Of Consul Metellus began to stir,
The causes of the war, its faults and ways,
    The game of Fortune and our leaders dire

Alliances, arms stained with unpurged blood,
    You treat, a work that's hazardous and rash;
And so you start your journey on a road
    Where hidden fires lurk under treacherous ash.

Now let the Muse of solemn tragedy
    Depart the theatre for a month or two!
Soon, when you have set out our history,
    You'll play great roles again on Attic shoe.

You were the sad defendants' eminent guard
    And of the Senate's high deliberations.
To you the laurel brought endless reward
    On your great triumph over the Dalmatians.

Again, now, with the cornet's loud menace
    You stun our ears. Again the clarion roars.
The flash of arms strikes fear in the knight's face
    And terrifies the swiftly flying horse.

And now I seem to hear those generals great,
    Their limbs with not inglorious dust defiled,
And the whole world submitting to defeat,
    Save Cato's spirit that refused to yield.

Juno and all the gods of Africa's shores
     Left their land unavenged. Once powerless,
She brought the grandsons of the conquerors
     To be Jugurtha's sacrificial mess.

What field has not grown fat with Latin blood,
     Where graves the price of impious wars attest,
The sound of ruin, which the Parthians heard,
     And Italy collapsing in the west?

What whirlpool and which river have not we
     Made witness to the woefulness of war?
Rome's corpses have discoloured every sea
     And Roman blood is there on every shore.

Abandon not your jests, my wayward Muse!
     Do not in Cean dirges take your fill!
Join me in Venus' grotto and then choose
     Some music that requires a lighter quill!

II.2
To Sallustius Crispus

Sallustius Crispus, no colour imbues
    Silver that's hidden in the miserly earth.
    You treat your coins as if they have no worth.
Just let them shine with reasonable use!

For generations, Proculeius' name
    Will live; he gave brothers a father's care.
    He will be borne, on wings that will not dare
To be unfastened, by undying Fame.

You'd reign more widely if you tamed your greed
    Than if you joined Libya with far Cadiz
    And Carthaginians on the sea's two sides
Submitted to what you alone decreed.

Through self-indulgence dreaded dropsy grows.
    Its thirst is not quenched till the origins
    Of the disease have run out from the veins
And listlessness from the white body flows.

Virtue dissents from all the common herds;
    Though Phraates is restored to Cyrus' throne,
    Yet of the blessed she numbers him not one,
For Virtue teaches men to shun false words.

Her kingdom and sure diadem she grants
    To him alone, with her own laurel wreath, –
    Whoever looks on massive piles of wealth
But passes on without a backward glance.

II.3
To Dellius

Keep a cool head when things are hard;
　　In good times curb excessive gladness!
For death will be your last reward,
　　Whether you live a life of sadness

Or, lying in the distant grass,
　　You sip your best Falernian wine
And toast the holidays that pass.
　　The white poplar and the great pine

Form love's alliance, and so marry
　　Branches to cover shady arbours;
The shimmering brook must never tarry,
　　As by the slanting bank it labours.

Here, send for wine and perfumes sweet,
　　The flowers of the rose soon dead,
While age and circumstance permit,
　　And the three Fates spin their black thread!

You'll leave the woodlands you did buy,
　　Your home, the farm yellow Tiber laps.
The wealth that you have piled up high
　　Your heir will drink. Though rich perhaps

And born of Inachus' ancient line,
　　Or poor and of the meanest caste
Of men under the heavens divine,
　　No matter! You will go at last,

A victim by cruel Orcus taken.
 We are all forced to the same fate;
The destiny of all is shaken
 In fortune's cup sooner or late.
Into eternal exile we
Shall go, on board the last ferry.

II.4
To Xanthias of Phocis

You love a slave girl. Do not be ashamed!
 Briseis was a slave, Achilles famed
For arrogance. And yet she could excite
 His love with her complexion of snow white.

Captive Tecmessa's beauty overawed
 The son of Telemon, Ajax her lord.
Atrides at his victory parade
 Burned for Cassandra, seized while yet a maid

After the Asian squadrons and their horse
 Fell to Thessalian victors, and the loss
Of Hector gave the weary troops of Greece
 A Troy that could be razed with greater ease.

Perhaps the parents of blond Phyllis are
 So rich you'd win status as son-in-law;
No doubt she still bemoans her royal blood
 And the injustice of her household god.

You can be sure the splendid girl you love
        Is not from the low classes and will prove
So trustworthy and so averse to gain,
        Her mother could not ever bring you shame.

Her arms, her face, her rounded calves I must
        Wholeheartedly commend. And don't distrust
Someone whose hastening seasons have now made
        Him close the door upon his fourth decade!

II.5
To Lalage's Admirer

She cannot with submissive neck support
        The yoke or do the duties of a mate,
And when the bull comes in for Venus' sport,
        She has no strength to tolerate his weight.

Your heifer's thoughts around green pastures roam;
        She cools the summer's heat where rivers flow,
Or, with the calves, enjoys her favourite game
        And gambols in a damp copse of willow.

That's what she now desires. Give up your passion
        For the unripe grape! Autumn will come for you
And blue-black clusters elegantly fashion,
        Picked out with highlights of deep crimson hue.

Soon she'll pursue you. Age runs savagely
        Apace and will tag onto her each year

That it subtracts from you. Soon Lalage
Seeking a husband will pertly appear.

She'll be more loved than fleeting Pholoe
Or Chloris with her shoulder gleaming white
As the pure moon that shimmers o'er the sea
Reflected in the waters of the night,

Or Gyges! If he joined a chorus line
Of girls, the obscure distinction would amaze.
Sage guests would be completely taken in
By his long hair and indeterminate face!

II.6
To Septimius

You hope to travel with me to Cadiz,
To Cantabrians who've not been taught to brave
Our yoke, and to the barbarous Syrtes
Where seethes incessantly the Moorish wave.

May Tibur, which an Argive settler founded,
Be home, I pray, for my advancing age!
By Tibur's limits may my life be bounded,
Weary of roads and war and sea voyage!

But if I'm kept away by hostile Fates,
I'll seek Galaesus' river sweet and cool
Where sheep go out in leather overcoats,
And fields Spartan Phalanthus used to rule.

That corner of the world still smiles for me
    More than all other places where men live.
Hymettus' mount has no sweeter honey
    Nor green Venafrum a more rich olive.

There, Jupiter affords long lasting springs
    And mild, warm winters. There, Mount Aulon's vines
Give fertile Bacchus friendly offerings
    And are not jealous of Falernian wines.

That fair location summons me and you
    Together. Us those blessed heights demand.
There, you will sprinkle with the tear that's due
    The glowing ashes of this bard your friend.

II.7
To Pompeius

Into the hour of death you often came
    With me, when Brutus led our soldiery.
Who has restored you to a citizen's name,
    Our fathers' gods and the Italian sky,

Pompeius, first of my comrades in arms?
    With you I often wore away with wine
The laggard day, and spread sweet Syrian balms
    Over my crowned locks to make them shine.

With you I felt Philippi and swift flight,
    Ingloriously leaving my small shield,
When manliness was shattered and the might
    Of youth fell chin-first on the shameful field.

Swift Mercury lifted me through the foe;
    In a thick mist my fearful frame he hid;
But back into the war you had to go,
    Sucked by the currents and the seething tide.

So give to Jove the banquet which you owe,
    Beneath my bay tree rest your weary side
Exhausted from your long campaign, and no,
    Spare not the wine jars that I've set aside!

Fill up the polished goblets to the brim
    With Massic wine that brings forgetfulness!
Pour out sweet unguents from the conch's rim
    In full measure! Who will make haste and dress

Garlands with myrtle or moist celery?
    Whom will the dice name Master of the Wine?
I'll outdo the Edonians' revelry.
    My friend is back: I want to lose my mind!

II.8
To Barine

If any punishment for broken faith
    Had ever brought you injury or distress,
If ever you were marred by a black tooth
    Or just one fingernail's slight ugliness,

I would believe you. But as soon as you
    Have bound with all those vows your faithless head,
You shine more brightly, with a beauty new,
    And young men ogle at your promenade.

At this show even Venus laughs, I say.
    The innocent Nymphs laugh; cruel Cupid, too,
Who on his bloodstained whetstone works away
    And hones his burning arrowheads anew.

Add this: a whole new generation grows
    To manhood for you, a fresh band of slaves;
And though they threaten to leave you, your old beaux
    Still court a mistress who impiously behaves.

At you, mothers of young bulls are in dread,
    And mean old men, who cling to their pennies,
And weeping brides, new to a husband's bed,
    In case their grooms are kept back by your breeze.

II.9
To Valgius

No, not for ever does the piercing rain
    Pour from the clouds onto foul fields below,
    Nor do the turbulent tempests always blow,
Tossing the surface of the Caspian main.

The still ice in Armenia does not last
    Or oak-woods groan in high Apulia
    Beneath the north wind twelve months in the year
And ash trees mourn the foliage that has passed.

Yet you with tearful music still dwell on
    Your lost Myrtes. Your love does not retire,
    Not at the rising of the evening star
Nor as it flees the fast approaching sun.

Nestor, whose life through three generations went,
    Mourned not Antilochus for all those years,
    And beardless Troilus' parents shed not tears
Nor did his Phrygian sisters all lament

For ever. It is time at last to cease
    All your effeminate weeping and wailing,
    And let us rather the new trophies sing
Of Augustus and the icebound Niphates;

How, added to the nations that now yield,
    The Medes' great river makes smaller whirlpools,
    And how Gelonians, kept within strict rules,
Now ride their horses on a petty field.

II.10
To Licinius

Your life would be in better shape
    If you stopped pressing out to sea
Or clinging too close to the rocky cape
    While eyeing storms too warily.

He, who adopts the golden mean,
    Safely avoids a squalid place
With a rotten roof, and isn't seen
    Courting envy in a grand palace.

The giant pine shakes most in the winds;
    The highest towers with the heaviest crash
Fall to the ground; the thunderstorm finds
    The topmost peaks with its lightning flash.

A heart that's learnt to anticipate
    In bad times hopes, in good will fear
The advent of the contrary fate.
    God, who brings back the winters drear,

Also dispels them. Today's bad news
    Won't last forever. Apollo
Can with his lyre wake a silent Muse;
    He does not always bend his bow.

When things are tight, be sure you're seen
    Spirited and brave! But if you're shrewd,
You'll draw your swollen sails right in
    Whenever the following wind's too good.

II.11
To Quinctius Hirpinus

What the warlike Cantabrians may conspire
    And Scythians over the Adriatic Sea,
Do not make it your purpose to enquire,
    And put aside all your anxiety

For life's requirements when life's wants are slight!
    Smooth-visaged youth and gracefulness retreat,
While, grey and withered, old age puts to flight
    The frolics of young loves and easy sleep.

The beauty of spring flowers does not remain,
    And the moon's face does not shine only red.
Why raise eternal questions once again
    And with them weary your inadequate head?

Beneath a lofty plane tree or this pine
    Why don't we, while we may, lie careless here,
And with grey hair rose-scented drink our wine
    And wallow in balm from Assyria?

Bacchus will soon dispel consuming care:
    We need a boy who's able to run fast
With goblets of Falernian wine on fire,
    To quench them in the fresh stream flowing past.

And who will go and lure out that shy tart,
    Lyde, from home? Go, tell her, no delay,
But bring her ivory lyre to play her part,
    Her hair tied in a knot, the Spartan way!

II.12
To Maecenas

The long and fierce Numantian war,
    Rough Hannibal and Punic blood
    Reddening the Sea of Sicily should
Not be themes for a soft guitar.

Wild Lapiths, Hylaeus drunk with wine,
    Earth's offspring tamed by Hercules' might,
    Whose exploits shook the shining bright
House of old Saturn divine,

No, not such themes; but you should write
    A prose account of Caesar's feats
    And menacing kings led through the streets
Dragged by the neck. That would be right!

My Muse has asked that I should tell
    Of sweet-singing Licymnia,
    A mistress' eyes that shine so clear,
A true heart for love shared so well.

How neatly she can dance, and play
    Her jokes and games, and throw her arms
    Round girls glowing with youthful charms
On thronged Diana's holiday.

The riches of Achaemenes
    Or Mygdon from fat Phrygia,
    Would you exchange for just one hair?
Or the Arabs' opulent palaces,

When she can bend her neck toward
        Your burning kisses, or deny
        Her love with easy cruelty?
Licymnia has always adored
    To have her kisses snatched with feeling,
        But sometimes likes to do the stealing!

II.13
To a Tree

Whoever planted you there first,
It was a day that was accursed,
And with a sacrilegious hand
He raised you, tree, so you would stand
A pest for grandchildren to come,
The village's opprobrium.
I would have thought that he could break
His father's or his mother's neck
And in his inmost sanctum could
Have spattered a guest's midnight blood.
He dealt in poisons from Colchis
And every other crime that is
Conceived in some or other way,
Planting you, timber of dismay,
To fall inside my own estate
On an innocent master's pate.
Those things, from which we should stay far,
We barely watch from hour to hour.
The Punic sailor fears the straits
Of Bosporus, but ignores the fates
That come from somewhere out of sight;

The soldier, arrows and the swift flight
Of Parthian cavalry, and they
The chains and jails of Italy.
But death's power, unforeseen till then,
Has snatched, and will, the tribes of men.
Now, I have virtually seen
The realms of dusky Proserpine,
The judgment seat of Aeacus,
The allotted home of the pious,
And Sappho who lamenting sings,
While plucking the Aeolian strings,
Of girls from her own island home,
And you, playing with gold plectrum,
Alcaeus, songs with fuller notes
Of hardships men suffer on boats,
The dreadful hardships they endure
In flight from battle and at war!
The shades attend each poet's word
That ought to be in silence heard,
But, with shoulders tight-packed, the throng
Drinks in more avidly the song
Of fighting, tyrants driven out.
What's there to be surprised about,
When songs on those subjects confound
The monstrous hundred-headed hound,
So that his dull, dark dog-ears droop
And poisonous vipers recoup
Their strength, all twisted at their ease
In the hair of the Eumenides?
Prometheus and Pelops' own sire
At the sweet playing of the lyre

Forget their toil, nor does Orion
Arouse the timorous lynx or lion.

II.14

To Postumus

"Eheu fugaces"

Alas, the fleeting years slip by,
    And wrinkles and insistent age
Won't be delayed by piety;
    Nor death that no man can assuage!

Not if three hundred bulls each day
    You sacrifice, will you placate
Cruel Pluto, whom no tears can sway
    And whose sad waves enclose the great

Geryon, thrice our human girth,
    And Tityos. We must all leave shore,
All who enjoy the fruits of earth,
    Whether we're kings or peasants poor.

What use to escape the wounds of war
    Or raucous breakers on the seas?
What use on autumn days to fear
    The southern wind that brings disease?

We must all see the languid flow
    Of errant Styx and the infamous throng
Of Danaus' daughters as we go,
    And Sisyphus damned to labours long.

We must leave our house, the land we till,
 Our pleasing wife; of these trees you tend,
None but the hated cypress will
 Follow their brief lord to the end.

A worthier heir will quaff the wine
 That with a hundred keys you stored,
And stain the floor with port too fine
 To be served at a pontiff's board.

II.15
The New Landscape

Soon, regal piles will leave few acres here
 For men to plough; on every side you'll see
Ponds stretching wider than the Lucrine mere,
 And everywhere the celibate plane tree

Will vanquish the elm. Soon, beds of violets and
 The myrtle and the nostrils' plenteous hoard
Will scatter their perfumes across the land
 Where olive groves enriched a former lord;

And laurel trees with branches cut and trained
 Will keep away the summer's burning blows. –
This was not what our ancestors ordained,
 Or Romulus' precepts and unshorn Cato's!

For them men's private wealth was brief and quick,
 The public coffers great. No columned porch

Was marked out with a private ten-foot stick
        To intercept winds from the shady north.

The laws did not allow them to dispense
        With casual turf, but made them give their towns
Enhancements at the Treasury's expense
        And decorate gods' temples with new stones.

II.16
To Grosphus

The sailor caught on the open sea
        Asks god for peace, as soon as cloud
        Has hidden the moon in a black shroud
And no stars shine with certainty.

Warring Thrace, furious and bold,
        The Mede armed with an ornate quiver,
        Seek peace, which gems cannot deliver
Nor raiment of purple, nor gold.

No treasure stores nor sheriff high
        Can shift the tumults of the mind
        Or clear away the cares unkind
That round the panelled ceilings fly.

A man lives well on little, whose
        Own father's saltcellar shines bright
        On a poor table and whose light
Sleep no fear or foul lust removes.

In our brief life man bravely tries
     So many shots. He changes one
     Place for lands warmed by another sun.
The exile from his own self flies.

False Care climbs up bronze battleships,
     Clings close behind squadrons of horse;
     Swifter than deer she runs her course,
Than Eurus who the rain clouds whips.

A heart that's happy for today
     Should hate to care for the morrow,
     Soothe bitterness with laughter slow;
Nothing is blessed in every way.

Swift death removed Achilles bright,
     Tithonus long senility
     Made weak, and the hour may offer me
That which it has to you denied.

A hundred herds around you call,
     Sicilian cows moo, and the mare
     Whinnies that pulls your four-horse car;
Twice dipped in African purple

Are your clothes. Honest Fate allowed
     Me a small farm, inspiration slight
     From the Greek Muses, and the right
To turn my back on the envious crowd.

II.17
To Maecenas

Why, why, Maecenas, do you drain my spirit
    With your complaints? Neither the gods nor I
    Will take pleasure if you are first to die,
Pillar of my affairs and badge of merit.

Oh, if indeed some premature duress
        Takes hold of you, a half of my own heart,
        Why do I then linger, the other part,
Surviving incomplete and valued less?

That day will end us both; I have declared
        No false allegiance. We shall go, shall go
        Wherever you shall lead, and we'll follow
Our supreme journey comrades well prepared.

Not if Chimaera's fiery breath awaits
        Or hundred-handed Gyas reappear,
        Will they tear me away from you, ever.
So decree potent Justice and the Fates.

No matter whether Libra looks on me,
        Or fearsome Scorpio who at the hour
        Of my birth had a more impetuous power,
Or Capricorn, king of the western sea,

The two of us have stars that correlate
        Incredibly; your glorious guardian,
        The planet Jupiter, from cursed Saturn
Snatched you and stayed the wings of flying Fate,

When in the theatre the assembled crowd
  Cheered you three times in acclamation glad;
  And I by a tree trunk falling on my head
Was carried off, had not Faunus allowed

His right hand to alleviate the blow,
  Protector of Mercury's friends. So bear in mind
  To offer victims and a votive shrine;
To sacrifice a humble lamb I'll go.

II.18
The Simple Life

No ivory, no gold panels shine
  Resplendent in a house of mine.
No roof beams from Hymettus weigh
  On columns hewn in Africa.
No unknown heir of Attalus
  Am I, seizing his royal palace.
For me no ladies of good birth
  Trail yards of purple Spartan cloth.
But good faith and a generous vein
  Of ingenuity are mine.
Though poor, I'm sought by rich men and
  Harass the gods with no demand.
I importune no powerful friend;
  I'm happy with my Sabine land.
Days are displaced by other days;
  New moons press on to end their phase;
You, to the death, contract for cut
  Marble and your own tomb forget.

You build houses and, where seas roar
   Against Baiae, push out the shore,
Pushing as if the wealth to hand
   Was held back by the bounds of land,
And you are constantly engrossed
   In tearing up the boundary post
On neighbouring fields and jumping o'er
   A client's fence, greedy for more, –
So man and wife, clutching grubby kids,
   Are driven out with their family gods!
No hall more certainly awaits
   A rich heir than the ordained gates
Of grasping Orcus. What's ahead?
   Earth opens equally for the dead,
The pauper and son of a king.
   Orcus' accomplice did not bring
Cunning Prometheus back to the world
   Seduced by bribes of solid gold.
Death can proud Tantalus confine,
   Imprison Tantalus's line.
Death relieves poor men, when they call
   And when they call not, from their toil.

II.19
Hymn to Bacchus

I saw Bacchus on distant crags repeat
     His songs – posterity believe me, please! –
     And Nymphs learning the words and melodies,
And Satyrs with pricked ears and goatish feet.

Oh, my brain shivers with this new alarm!
     My heart o'erbrims with Bacchus! He fills me
     With turbulent joy. Oh, Liber, let me be!
Let not your heavy baton do me harm!

I must sing of the untiring Thyiades,
     A fountainhead of wine, a copious stream, –
     Duty requires me! – flowing with rich cream,
And honey dripping down the hollow trees.

Of Ariadne, your own blessed bride
     Who added lustre to the stars, I sing;
     Of Pentheus' high roof's merciless shattering,
And how the King of Thrace Lycurgus died.

You bend the rivers and the barbarous sea;
     In far-off mountain ranges, drunk with wine,
     You weave the vipers into knotted twine
And bind the Bistonids' tresses' harmlessly.

When the impious gang of giants went to war
     And scaled the heights to reach your father's doors,
     You hurled back Rhoetus with a lion's claws
And beat him off with your horrendous jaw.

Although you have been spoken of as more
          Suited for dancing and for sport and jest,
          And, by repute, for battle not the best,
Yet you held centre stage in peace and war.

Cerberus watched you innocently, complete
          With your gold horn. He rubbed his tail along
          Your side with soft strokes; then, with triple tongue,
He licked your legs and your departing feet.

II.20
Epilogue

No, on no frail or ordinary wing
    Shall I be borne aloft through empty space,
A bard of double form, nor shall I cling
    Too long to earth, but rise above the place

Of envy and leave cities far beneath.
    I am of poor men's blood. You call, I go!
Yet, dear Maecenas, I shall not face death,
    Nor be imprisoned by the Stygian flow.

Now on my legs a rough patch of skin gathers;
    Above, I change into a pure white swan,
As on my shoulders appear nascent feathers
    And on my fingers a smooth coat of down.

More famed than Daedalus' son Icarus,
    I'll be a bird of song, and I'll fly forth
To view the shores of groaning Bosporus,
    Moroccan sands and cold plains of the north.

They'll know me in Colchis, in far Ukraine,
    Romania, where they refuse to tell
Their fear of Latin troops; learn me in Spain
    By heart, and where Rhone's river-drinkers dwell.

At such an unreal funeral let's have
    No dirge or ugly mourning or lament!
No acclamation, please, but at my grave
    Let all superfluous honours be absent!

Book III

III.1
The Unholy Throng

I loathe the unholy throng and I have barred
    Them entry. Hold your tongues, and no more noise!
For I sing songs that ne'er before were heard –
    A priest of Muses, I – for girls and boys.

Though awesome kings control the flocks they own,
    The kings themselves are ruled by supreme God.
Jove's conquest of the Giants won him renown;
    He moves the universe with but a nod.

One man in broader lines may regulate
    His orchard, one with a more fine surname
May stroll downhill to be a candidate
    Upon the Campus, one compete through fame

And character; and one may have a host
    Of clients. Impartial Necessity
Draws lots of both the best and nethermost;
    The vast urn shakes names in totality.

For the evil man, who sees a drawn sword raised
    Above his neck, Sicilian banquets are
Unable to bring out their long sweet taste,
    And melodies of birdsong and guitar

Bring no sleep; soft sleep, creeping o'er the bed
    Of country folk, is never so unkind
To humble homes and river banks in shade
    Or Tempe's valley fanned by the west wind.

The man, who only wants what is enough,
    Is not disturbed by the tumultuous sea,
By Arcturus' descent so wild and rough
    Or by the rising kid-star's savagery,

No, not by vineyards lashed by beating hail,
    Or a mendacious farm whose trees reproach
First rain, then constellations that assail
    And parch the fields, then unfair winter's touch.

Meanwhile, the fishes feel the waters shrink
    As piles drive into the deep. A busy band
Of contractors and their employees sink
    Thick rubble for a lord who scorns the land.

But Fear and Menace clamber upward now
    To the lord's mansion. Black Anxiety
Sits on the trireme with the brazen prow
    And behind the horseman as he rides away.

So, if the troubled mind can find no calm
    In Phrygian marble, star-bright purple clothes,
Or in the most expensive Persian balm
    Or in Falernian vineyards, why suppose

That I would want to build in the latest style
    A hilltop palace with a swanky gate?
Why would I wish to change my Sabine vale
    For riches that were more elaborate?

III.2
"Dulce et decorum"

Hardship and poverty let him but bear,
    The boy who's been toughened by service for war;
Let him learn them and welcome them, then ride and go
    To harry the ferocious Parthian foe!

Let the Parthians quake at this knight and his spear;
    Let him live under heaven and dare without fear!
On the enemy ramparts the queen from on high
    Will gaze, and her daughter the princess will sigh,

As her father the tyrant is warring below:
    "May this prince of my heart, oh this unseasoned foe,
Not provoke the fierce lion that blood-lust and wrath
    Drive on through a chaos of carnage and death!"

To die for one's country is glorious and sweet;
    Death chases the runaway, however fleet;
It spares not the youth who is scared to attack,
    But sunders his hams and his cowardly back.

Manliness knows of no sordid retreat
    And untarnished honours lie bright at its feet;
Nor accepts nor resigns any office to please
    The judgment that goes with the popular breeze.

Manliness finds a new way to the sky,
    Unlocking a road for men too good to die;
It shuns common gatherings, the earth's soil that clings,
    And flies up to heaven on vanishing wings.

And yet loyal silence has also its due;
　　　The countryside's secrets are sacred. He, who
Dares publish them, won't stay beneath the same beams
　　　Or share my canoe with me on country streams!

The Almighty, neglected, is not always sure
　　　To draw a distinction between impure and pure,
But club-footed Punishment, time after time,
　　　Catches up with the man who's committed a crime.

III.3
Juno's Declaration

The man, who is just and clings to his intent,
　　　No fiery braying of the electorate,
No threatening tyrant's glare, will make relent
　　　From his resolve; not Auster, the unquiet

Adriatic's stormy general, nor e'en
　　　The mighty hand of thunder-flashing Jove.
Oh, if the shattered firmament fell in
　　　And ruins rained on him, he would fearless prove.

So Pollux and the wandering Hercules
　　　Strove to attain the pinnacles of fire,
Between whom Augustus will lie at ease
　　　And sip with crimson lips divine nectar.

So, father Bacchus, honouring your deeds,
    Your untrained tigers took the yoke and sped
Aloft with you. So, too, on Mars's steeds
    Quirinus fled the kingdom of the dead.

Then, Juno uttered words none could begrudge
    To the assembled gods: "Ah, Ilium!
How fatal, how unchaste has been the judge
    Who with that wandering woman has now come

"To turn Troy into dust, its doom e'er since
    Laomedon stole from the gods divine
Their promised price! Troy, people, fraudulent prince,
    Condemned to chaste Minerva's care and mine!

"No longer does the infamous guest have charms
    For Sparta's adultress, nor perjured house
Of Priam break the Achaeans and their arms
    By virtue of great Hector and his powers.

"The war, which our own feuds served to create,
    Is settled. So, forthwith, my anger sore
And that grandson of mine, whom I do hate
    And whom Troy's priestess Rhea Silvia bore,

"I will give back to Mars; I shall allow
    Him to enter these seats of the luminous sky,
Sip juices of nectar and be entered now
    Within the peaceful ranks of gods on high.

"So long as there stretches the savage main
       Between defeated Ilium and Rome,
Let the blessed exiles choose their place to reign!
       So long as cattle trample on Priam's tomb

"And Paris's, and the wild beasts unharmed
       Still hide their cubs there, let the Capitol stand
Refulgent, and let Rome ferociously armed,
       Give vanquished Asians her lawful command!

"And may Rome spread her dreaded name afar
       To the world's ends, where the intermediate strait
Divides Europe from men of Africa,
       And swollen Nile waters its fields of wheat.

"Gold undiscovered, Rome will dare refuse,
       Esteeming more that which the earth conceals,
Rather than forcing it to human use
       With a right hand that all things sacred steals.

"Whatever bound is set upon the world,
       She'll touch it with her might, eager to view
The regions where the revelling fires have whirled
       And realms of mist and fog and rainy dew.

"But to the warlike Romans I declare
       The fates with this proviso: not to enjoy
Such piety or faith as to repair
       The rooftops of their own ancestral Troy.

"Then, born again with omens of sad weeping,
   Troy's fortune will repeat her loss of life;
Greek troops victorious will be in my keeping,
   And am I not Jove's sister and his wife?

"And if Troy thrice rebuilt a brazen wall
   At Phoebus' instigation, thrice again
Would it be cut down by my Greeks and fall,
   And captive wives would mourn their sons and men."

This topic does not suit the cheerful lyre.
   What is your purpose, wilful Muse? Please finish!
The gods' discourses only serve to tire,
   And great themes with poor music you diminish.

III.4
In Praise of the Muse

Come down from heaven, Calliope,
   And on your flute a long tune play!
Sing with high voice, if you prefer;
   Pluck Phoebus' strings, play his guitar!

Can you all hear sweet madness play
   With me? I seem to hear and stray,
Wandering through the hallowed trees
   Filled with fair waters and the breeze.

On the Apulian mount Voltur
    Outside my nursemaid Pullia's door,
Tired from my play, a sleeping child,
    On me magic ringdoves piled

Fresh leaves, a miracle revealed
    To all who dwell in the low weald
Of Forentum, glades of Bantia
    Or nest of high Acherontia.

Mid deadly snakes and bears I slept
    Safely, my infant body kept
In gathered myrtle and sacred bay,
    And blessed with heavenly bravery.

Muses, I'm yours when I behold
    The Sabine heights, Praeneste cold,
Or if the slopes of Tibur please
    Or Baiae with her limpid seas.

Dear to your springs and dancing, I
    Survived the rout of Philippi,
The fall of the accursed tree,
    Shipwreck and waves from Sicily.

With you beside me, I would sail
    The straits of Bosporus in a gale
And dare to walk the burning sands
    Along Assyria's coastal lands.

Inhospitable Britons I would
    Brave, Basques drunk on horse's blood,
Ukrainians with quivers armed,
    The Scythian river, – quite unharmed!

When high Augustus craves an end
    Of labours and decides to send
His weary troops back home on leave,
    You heal him in your Pierian cave.

You give soft counsel and rejoice
    When it is given. The impious
Titans and the Giants' revolt
    Were quelled by the falling thunderbolt

Of him who tempers windy seas,
    Still earth, the sad realms, great cities, –
One monarch who with even sway
    Rules gods and mortal cavalry.

Then, trusting in their ham-like arms,
    The young Giants brought Jove great alarms;
The brothers, too, who tried to drop
    Pelion on dark Olympus' top.

What could Typhoeus, Mimas strong
    Or Porphyrion who threatened wrong,
Rhoetus, or Enceladus do,
    Who tore up trees or boldly threw,

When they rushed at the ringing shield
    Of Pallas? Here, keen Vulcan held
His ground; here, Jove's own wife Juno
    And he who'll never rest his bow,

Apollo (who washes his long hair
    In pure dews from Castalia)
Of Delos, Patara, Lycia's thorn
    And native woods where he was born.

Brute force collapses by its weight.
    The gods raise force that's moderate
To greater power; at the same time,
    They hate force bent on every crime.

One-hundred-handed Gyas is
    A witness to my homilies;
Diana's tempter, Orion famed,
    By her virgin arrow tamed!

Thrown on her own monsters, Earth
    Mourns sons to whom she gave birth,
All dispatched by thunderbolt
    To the lurid underworld.

The swift fire from grim Orcus
    Cannot eat through Etna's mass;
Tityos' jailer with stretched wings
    Chews his liver for his sins.
The lover Pirithous remains
Imprisoned by three hundred chains.

III.5
The Example of Regulus

When Jupiter is thundering in the sky,
      We all believe that he is king above;
Augustus, when Britons and Persians lie
      Beneath his sway, a present god will prove.

Did Crassus' soldiers live to be debased
      By foreign wives, by enemies taken in –
Morals perverted and Senate disgraced! –
      To grow old under arms with their wives' kin,

And Marsians and Apulians conform
      To Persian rule, forgetting the holy shields,
Their name, eternal Vesta, uniform,
      While Jove was unharmed and Rome never yields?

This, Regulus resisted with foresight,
      Vowing to shameful terms not to succumb,
And demonstrating the contingent blight
      Upon a generation yet to come,

If Rome's young soldiers were not left to die
      Captive, unpitied. "Our standards attached
To Punic shrines I've seen; our weaponry,"
      Said he, "from our men without bloodshed snatched!

"I've seen the arms of Roman citizens tied
      Behind the backs that once knew freedom's taste,
And unbarred gates and tilled fields have I spied,
      That once by Roman soldiers were laid waste.

"I guess a soldier, when redeemed for gold,
           Comes back the braver! You would just add cost
To the disgrace. Re-dyeing wool that's old
           Does not restore the colours that are lost,

"Nor does true manliness, when once it's gone,
           Care much to be replaced in weaker men.
Do deer in thickly woven nets fight on
           When extricated? He'll be valiant then,

"Who entrusted himself to perfidious foes,
           And crush them in the next Punic campaign,
When he feared death, and submissively chose
           To feel their thongs his own forearms restrain?

"Since he knew not how life was truly gained,
           He confused peace with war. Shame, shame! I cry.
For you, great Carthage, greater heights attained
           Upon the infamous ruins of Italy."

It's said that Regulus threw off the embrace
           Of his good wife, put his small children by,
As though stripped of his rank, set his manly face
           And turned toward the ground a downcast eye,

Till with unique advice he won the day;
           Strength to the tottering Senate he restored
And, mid his grieving friends, without delay
           In honourable exile went abroad.

Although he knew of all the preparations
    That the barbarian torturer had made,
He pushed aside the throng of his relations,
    And populace who his return delayed,

As if, after a lengthy day in court
    On clients' business, when the suit had come
To its determination, he now sought
    Venafrum's fields or Spartan Tarentum.

III.6
Rome's Moral Decline

Roman, though guiltless, you must now atone
    For your forefathers' crimes, till you remake
The shrines and temples that are falling down
    And the images polluted with black smoke.

You rule the world through fealty to heaven:
    The gods are all beginning and all end.
When they have been ignored, the gods have given
    Misfortunes that sad Italy could not mend.

Twice did Monaeses and Pacorus' band
    Crush our assaults, which the auguries had scorned,
And twice took spoils of war from Roman hand
    And with them their mean necklaces adorned.

When we were in the grip of civil war,
  Our Ethiopian and Dacian foes
Almost sacked Rome, one with a fleet to fear,
  One mightier with volleys of arrows.

That century, fertile and fat with sin,
  First soiled our marriages and homes and race;
From this fount devastation flooded in
  Onto our fatherland and populace.

The ripe young virgin thrills now, as she learns
  Ionian dance, and with an artist's skills
Fashions herself; for unchaste love she yearns,
  When she still has a baby's fingernails!

And soon she looks out for adulterous boys,
  While her own husband in his wine delights,
Nor does she choose who'll snatch forbidden joys
  As her gift when the slaves remove the lights,

But there, before her husband's knowing eyes,
  She rises at the call of the entrepreneur
Or Spanish sea captain; they buy their prize
  And pay good prices to dishonour her.

Not from these parents came the brave offspring
  Who stained the sea with Carthaginian blood
And struck down Pyrrhus and the mighty king
  Antiochus and Hannibal the dread.

No, they were rustic soldiers' manly stock,
> Who used the Sabine hoe to turn the soil

And from strict mothers their instructions took,
> To cut down timber and endure the toil

Of carrying logs, while the declining sun
> Altered the mountain shades and brought the hour

For yokes to be released from tired oxen –
> A happy time! – with his departing car.

Time's ravages diminish everything.
> Worse than our forebears' was our fathers' age;

We are more wicked, and we shall soon bring
> A more defective future heritage.

III.7
To Asterie

Why do you weep? The fair west wind
> Will bring back your love in the early spring;
> Piles of exotic wares he'll bring,

Unbroken faith and a constant mind.

The south wind took him to Oricum:
> First came the autumn's mad Goat Star,
> Now sleepless he sheds many a tear,

For winter's freezing nights have come.

An anxious hostess's messenger:
　　　　"Chloe's sad and sighs and burns," he says, –
　　　　With fires like yours! – in a thousand ways
Seducing him to follow her.

He tells of a false wife's slanderous lie
　　　　Driving credulous Proteus on,
　　　　And all-too-chaste Bellerophon
Dispatched by him in haste to die,

And Peleus, almost carried in
　　　　To Tartarus, when he chose to flee
　　　　Rather than touch Hippolyte,
And false tales that teach men to sin.

In vain! For your lover, at his voice,
　　　　Is deafer than rocks in the sea, and pure,
　　　　Until now! But you must beware!
Don't fall for your neighbour Enipeus!

There's no one else who steers a horse
　　　　So skilfully on the Field of Mars,
　　　　And no one else who swims so fast
Along the Tuscan river's course.

Lock your house at dusk, and don't look down
　　　　To the street at the song of the querulous flute!
　　　　And though he may often call you rude,
Just keep responding with a frown!

III.8
To Maecenas

What am I doing, you ask, a bachelor
    On this the first of March? What are they for,
The flowers, the box of incense and the coal
    Piled up on a grass altar? You, the soul

Of scholarship in Latin and Greek lore!
    I promised a sweet banquet and a pure
White kid to Liber, when I was nearly
    Sent to my grave by the blow of a falling tree.

Today's a happy anniversary which
    Will draw a cork that has been sealed with pitch
From an old wine jar ageing by the grate
    Since Lucius Volcacius' consulate.

So take a hundred ladlesful, please do,
    To celebrate your own dear friend's rescue!
Light up the lanterns till the light of day!
    Let noise and anger both be far away!

Don't let the cares of state enter your head;
    The troops of Dacian Cotiso are dead,
And Parthian from Parthian dissents,
    All waging war with dismal armaments.

Our old Cantabrian foe from shores of Spain
    Is tamed for servitude with a late chain;
The Scythians unstring their curved bow
    And contemplate leaving the plains below.

Relax! A private citizen should not care
     Too much what burdens the nation may bear.
Enjoy the glad gifts of this festive tide
     And put your serious worries to one side!

III.9
The Poet and Lydia

"As long as I was your delight
     And there was no more potent youth to fling
His arms around your neck so white,
     I lived more blessed than a Persian king!"

"As long as for none else you burned
     And Lydia was not Chloe's inferior,
Though many other heads I turned,
     I lived more glorious than Rome's Ilia!"

"I'm ruled now by Thracian Chloe,
     Skilled in sweet music, good at the guitar!
For her I'd not be afraid to die,
     If only fate would grant more years to her!"

"We blaze with mutual torches, I
     And Calais the boy from Thurium!
For him I'd willingly twice die,
     If only fate would grant more years to him!"

"What if our old Venus returned
   And bound with a bronze yoke two she'd split before;
If flaxen-haired Chloe were spurned
   And jilted Lydia found an open door?"

"Though he's more beautiful than a star,
   And you lighter than cork and more angry
Than the rough sea of Hadria,
   With you I'd love to live, and gladly die."

III.10
To Lyce

If you drank from the furthest Tanais,
     A savage for a husband, still you'd cry
To see me battered by the indigenous
     North wind, as I lay in your rough alley.

Can you not hear how noisily your door
     And spinney that between fair rooftops grows
Groan at the bellowing wind, as Jupiter
     With pure divinity freezes the snows?

This haughtiness, which Venus hates, eschew,
     Lest on the wheel the rope should backward fly;
You're no Penelope that none can woo
     Or daughter of Etrurian gentry!

Although you bend neither to gift nor prayer
    Nor lovers' pallor touched with violet hue,
Nor at your smitten husband's love affair
    With a Thessalian, spare your suppliant true,

Though you're less pliant than a winter oak,
    Your heart less gentle than a Moorish snake!
No, not forever shall the heavens soak
    My suffering bones that on your doorstep ache.

III.11
To Mercury and the Lyre

Mercury, who once in Amphion found
    An apt pupil, who moved the stones with song;
    And Tortoiseshell, you who have practised long
With seven strings to make your tunes resound,

Though silent once and glum, yet now so dear
    To temples and the tables of the rich:
    Tell us the measures and music, to which
Lyde must now apply her obdurate ear;

For she's a filly, a young three year old
    Cavorting on the plain, an innocent
    Fearing man's touch and nuptial blandishment,
Still unripe for a rough husband to hold.

You can lead tigers and attendant trees,
        And stay the course of rivers as they race.
        The monstrous gatekeeper of the palace
Has yielded to your charming melodies,

Dread Cerberus, although a hundred snakes
        Defend that head which the fierce Furies know,
        And noxious breath and foul gore ooze and flow,
As from his mouth his triple tongue he takes.

Once, even Ixion and Tityos
        Gave an unwilling smile, and the urn stood dry
        A brief while, when your welcome lullaby
Delighted the daughters of Danaus.

Let Lyde hear the crimes of these young maids,
        Their famous punishment, the empty vase
        With water disappearing from the base,
And the late Fates, who even among the shades

For culpable offences lie in wait.
        Those impious girls, what could they do more vile?
        Those impious girls took toughened pins of steel
The murder of their grooms to perpetrate.

One out of many worthy of marriage
        And honouring its flame by perjury
        Addressed her father with a splendid lie,
A maid noble to every future age.

To her young husband, "Rise," she said, "and leave!
    Arise, in case the long sleep you yearn for
    Comes from an unfeared source! Your father-in-law
And my foul sisters you must now deceive.

"Like lionesses lighting on bull calves,
    They're tearing them apart, ah! one by one!
    I am more gentle. I'll not strike you down
Or hold you captive behind prison bars.

"Let Father weigh me down with his cruel chains
    For sparing my poor spouse with clemency!
    Let him command his fleet to banish me
To far Numidia's remotest plains!

"Go where your feet lead and the breezes flee,
    While Night befriends you and the Queen of Love!
    Go with fair omens, and an epitaph
Carve on my tomb in memory of me!"

III.12
To Neobule

It is not done
    for poor girls to play
At romantic fun,
    wash their cares away

Drinking sweet wine
     or pass out in fear
Of an uncle's tongue-
     lashing in their ear.

Winged Cupid
     has been thieving
Your wool-basket;
     and your weaving
And your picks and ends
     are off duty,
For your boyfriend's
     such a beauty:

He oils his shoulders
     and dives straightaway
In the Tiber's cold to
     wash the oil away!
A better rider
     than Bellerephon!
Boxer, sprinter,
     he is quite alone!

In the open field,
     when the herd's hot
And the stags flee,
     he's a top shot!
When a boar's crept
     into dense brush
He can intercept
     at a fair rush!

III.13
The Bandusian Spring

Spring of Bandusia more bright than glass,
  Honoured with pure sweet wine and flowers afloat,
  Tomorrow you'll be given a billy goat,
His forehead swollen with the earliest press

Of horns that forecast love and war, – in vain!
  For this offspring of the lascivious herd
  Is destined to spill out his crimson blood
And dye your ice cold currents with the stain.

The blazing dog days at their fiercest hour
  Can't touch you with their violence; you know how
  To give warm cold to bulls tired from the plough
And cattle that come wandering from afar.

Of all the noble springs you'll win renown,
  When I tell of the oak tree on your ridge
  Of hollow rocks, and your clear waters which
Chatter away as they come tumbling down.

III.14
To the Common People of Rome

Like Hercules, Augustus sought the rewards
  Of laurel wreaths that death alone can buy,
But Caesar has returned to his own gods
  From Spanish shores that gave him victory.

His wife, rejoicing at her unique lord,
>   Shall after sacred rituals appear;
The sister of our emperor adored,
>   The ladies wearing holy bands of prayer,

And mothers of young men and maidens who
>   Have now been saved. You boys, and girls who wait
In untried innocence for a husband true,
>   Refrain from words that tempt an evil fate.

Today is truly a holiday for me
>   And it will drive all my dark worries forth;
I'll fear no strife, I'll not be afraid to die
>   A violent death, while Caesar owns the earth.

Go, find unguents, my boy! Find crowns for us,
>   A wine jar that recalls the Marsian war
Or earthen flask that rebel Spartacus
>   Amid his many wanderings never saw!

Go, tell Neaera with her voice so gay
>   To bind her perfumed hair in a quick knot,
But if you find that there is some delay
>   Caused by the hateful porter, homeward trot!

Spirits grow gentler as the hair goes white,
>   When they once loved quarrels and brawls uncouth;
I could not, during Plancus' consulate,
>   Have suffered this in the hot flush of youth!

III.15
To Chloris

You are just a poor man's wife
      Living an immoral life;
Now it's time for you to shirk
      All your infamous hard work.
As you near your dying day,
      You must now retire from play
Among the girls; you must desist
      From blanketing bright stars with mist.
What suits Pholoe well enough
      May on you, my dear, look rough;
It's more proper for your daughter
      To lead young men to the slaughter,
Like a Bacchante in their home
      Roused by a pulsating drum.
Now love's new compulsions bid
      Her frolic like a frisky kid;
Wool from famed Luceria
      Makes you seem superior.
You're not suited by guitars
      Or the rose's scarlet flowers
Or, now you're on your last legs,
      Magnums drunk down to the dregs!

III.16
To Maecenas

For captive Danae a tower of bronze
    And doors of strong oak and the dismal sight
Of watchful dogs without, had been defence
    Enough from the seducers of the night,

Had not Acrisius, who jailed the maid,
    Been mocked by Jove and Venus for his fear.
If gods were turned into a bribe, they said,
    The journey would be safe, the pathway clear.

Gold loves to travel through the midst of guards
    And break through rocks with more power than the blow
Of thunderbolts. By love of rich rewards
    The house of the Argive prophet was brought low.

The Macedonian burst through city gates
    And undermined with bribes his rival kings;
And bribes ensnare the captains of frigates,
    Entangling rough commanders with their strings.

Increasing wealth creates anxiety
    And hunger for still more; I have been right
Not to expose my crest conspicuously,
    Maecenas, glorious and distinguished knight.

The more that each man has himself denied,
    The more he'll have from heaven. Naked I've sought
To cross the lines and flee the wealthy side,
    And reach the camp of those who desire naught,

The lord of a despised estate more blessed
    Than if I hid within my granary store
All that the tough Apulians could harvest:
    Amid great riches I am richly poor.

A stream of water pure, a modest wood
    And certain faith in my own cornfield are
A happier lot that shining consuls could
    Enjoy when governing fertile Africa.

I have no honey from Calabrian bees;
    No wine in Laestrygonian jars matures
For me to drink; no sheep grow a thick fleece
    While grazing on my lush Gallic pastures.

Yet cruel poverty is far away
    And, if I wanted more, you'd not refuse.
Reducing my desires, I surely may
    Better extend my tiny revenues

Than if I added to the Mygdon plains
    Alyattes' kingdom. Those who look for much
Lack much. He's happy who from heaven gains
    A sparing handful of what is enough.

III.17
To Aelius Lamia

Aelius, after old Lamus nobly named,
    From him, it's said, your forebears proudly claimed
Their surname, and authentic records show
    That all their later generations flow

From that sole origin, who many say
    Was first to own the walls of Formiae
And River Liris swimming 'twixt the shores
    Marica loves, – a tyrant prince with powers

Spread far and wide. Tomorrow, the woodland
    Will be covered in leaves, and the sea strand
With useless seaweed will be overstrewn
    By a rain storm that the east wind has sent down,

Unless rain's harbinger, the ancient crow
    Deceives me. While you can, gather dry wood, now!
Tomorrow you'll release your staff from work
    And celebrate with mulled wine and roast pork.

III.18
Hymn to Faunus

Faunus, the Nymphs flee at your love:
    Across my bounds and country fair
Walk soft and, when you onward move,
    Protect the small ones in my care!

A tender kid at the year's end
    Is yours for this; wines to o'erbrim
The deep bowl that is Venus' friend,
    And the old altar's smoky perfume.

The herd plays in the grassy leas
    On your special December day,
And in the fields the ox takes his ease
    And villagers have a holiday.

Mid fearless lambs the wolf now strays;
    For you leaves from the wild woods fall;
The ditch digger gives three hurrays
    And stamps upon the hated soil.

III.19
To Telephus

How many years there are from Inachus
    To Codrus who was not afraid to die
For his country, the tribe of Aeacus,
    The wars fought under Ilium's sacred sky,

All this you tell. The price of Chian wines
    And who will warm the water on the flame,
When I'll be rid of the chill of the Apennines,
    And who'll be host, none of this can you name.

Now pour a toast for the new moon, young man,
    A toast to midnight, quick! A toast of wine
To Murena the Augur! Our cups can
    Be mixed with three full ladles or with nine!

The inspired bard who loves the uneven Muses
    Will thrice three ladles in the bowl demand,
For more than three our Grace strictly refuses,
    Dancing with her nude sisters hand in hand!

She fears a quarrel; I like to go mad!
    Why has the pipe of Berecyntia
Ended its blasts? Why is the flute unplayed
    Hanging adjacent to the silent lyre?

I hate right hands that are ungenerous:
    Scatter the rose petals! Let Lycus hear
Our crazy din and make an old man's fuss, —
    His ill-matched lady, too, our neighbour fair!

Your hair is thick, Telephus, and you glow;
    You're as unsullied as the evening star.
Rhoda's in bloom for you and wants you so.
    I burn with slow love for my Glycera!

III.20
To Pyrrhus

Don't you see that a lioness,
Whose cub's disturbed, is dangerous?
A timid huntsman, you'll soon flee
War's hardships, when through a company
Of hostile youths she goes to seek
Nearchus, the outstanding Greek.
A mighty contest it will be,
Whether you win the prize or she!

But as swift arrows you unsheathe
And she whets her horrendous teeth,
The innocent umpire of the bout
Has trampled the palm underfoot
(We hear) and the soft wind caresses
His shoulder beneath perfumed tresses,
Like Nereus or fair Ganymede
Snatched from Ida's wet mountainside.

III.21
For Corvinus
(To a Wine Jar)

O sister, born in the same year as I,
Who brings dejection or hilarity,
Quarrels or the insanity of love
Or easy sleep: holy wine jar, approve
Whatever name we give you to preserve
Your Massic! On a holiday you deserve
A move. Come down! Corvinus wants to pour
A wine that is more mellow and mature.

He won't ignore you and he won't be rude,
Though with Socratic discourse he's imbued;
It's said e'en Cato's manliness grew hot
In olden times when he had drunk a lot!
So, to the character that's quite austere
You bring your gentle torment; you lay bare
The wise man's cares and his secret design
For jesting Bacchus, the easy god of wine.

You bring back hope to minds that are unsure,
Strength to the anxious, horns to help the poor,
Who, after you, fear not the angry intent
Of crested kings or soldiers' armament.
Now Liber and glad Venus will come by,
The Graces will their tardy knots untie,
And living lanterns will prolong your hours
Till Phoebus comes to chase away the stars.

III.22
To Diana

Guard of the mountains, Virgin of the grove,
　　　When brides endure the travails of the womb,
Thrice called you hear their cries and you remove
　　　Them from death's grasp, goddess of triple form!

Above my farmhouse, let the pine be yours!
　　　There, every passing year in joyous mood,
I'll take a pig and, as it measures its force
　　　For an angled strike, I will donate its blood.

III.23
To Phidyle

If you have raised open hands to the sky
　　　At the moon's birth, and made your gods a vow
With incense and the year's crops, Phidyle,
　　　My country girl, and killed a greedy sow,

The pestilent wind from Africa won't harm
　　　Your fertile vine, and sterile mildew shall
Not blight the harvest, nor sweet kid or lamb
　　　Feel the harsh weather in the fruitful fall.

A victim nourished in Algidus' snows
　　　Between the oak trees and the tall ilex,
Or one that in the Alban grasses grows,
　　　Will stretch its neck and stain the pontiff's axe

In sacrifice: it's not for you to try
      With vast slaughter to tempt small deities,
Whom you already crown with rosemary
      And garlands of delicate myrtle leaves.

An innocent hand, that's to the altar come,
      Needs no rich sacrifice to allay its fault,
But mollifies the unhearing gods of home
      With holy flour and jumping grains of salt.

III.24
Rome's Immorality

Though wealthier than the untapped stores
    Of Arabs and rich India's shores,
And though you fill the whole Tuscan sea
    And Adriatic with debris,
Since dire Necessity can fix
    Her steel spikes to the highest peaks,
From fear you won't set your mind loose
    Or free your head from death's tight noose.
The Scythians, who on flat plains roam
    As wagons pull their wandering home,
Live better, and the stiff Getae,
    Whose unallotted lands give free
Produce and cereal all can share,
    Though cultivated year to year;
Each in his turn does equal toil
    For one who's finished with the soil;
There, orphaned stepchildren can find
    A mother innocent and kind;

No dowried wife rules husband poor
    Nor trusts a polished paramour, –
Her dowry's the morality
    Her parents gave, the chastity
That fears strange loves and has sure faith:
    To sin is wrong, the price is death!
He, who will end this impious age
    Of carnage and of civil rage,
If he wants statues with the name
    "Father of Cities," may he tame
Our unchecked immorality
    And win fame from posterity!
We hate pure virtue in our sin,
    But at its absence we complain.
What is the point of sad lament,
    If guilt's not pruned by punishment?
What has vain legislation done,
    When all morality is gone,
If lands the burning fires enclose,
    Latitudes where the north wind blows,
Or snow grown hard upon the ground
    Can't keep the merchant from his round,
And crafty sailors rule the main,
    And poverty brings great disdain
And makes us all things bear and do,
    And leaves the path of steep virtue?
Let's throw into the Capitol,
    Where massed ranks of supporters call,
Or into the nearest ocean hurl
    Our useless gold, each gem and pearl,
The substance of our greatest ill,
    If true repentance we can feel.

All elements of depraved lust
    Must be uprooted; weak minds must
Be moulded with training more tough.
    The freeborn boy, awkward and rough,
Can't ride a horse and hold his mount;
    He's not only afraid to hunt,
He plays expertly, if you please,
    With Greek hoops and illegal dice.
His father's perjury up-ends
    A business partner and his friends,
So he can pile up cash in haste
    For his unworthy heir to waste.
Dishonest riches build and build,
    But deficits are still revealed!

III.25
To Bacchus

Where do you take me, as I rave?
    To what wood am I taken, or cave?
My head feels strange, I move at speed;
    On what high rock shall I be heard,
Telling the stars and gods the story
    Of great Caesar's perpetual glory?
I'll tell a new and noted truth
    Untold by any other mouth.
The sleepless Bacchante on the height
    Looks out amazed at snowy white
Thrace and River Hebrus' flood
    And Rhodope crossed by foreign foot.

So, too, as I wander, I love
  The river banks and empty grove.
O king of Naiads, Bacchantes, too,
  Who the high ash trees overthrew,
I'll not mean words or humbly speak,
  Nothing mortal! It's danger sweet,
Bacchus, to follow a god divine,
  My head wreathed with green shoots of vine.

III.26
Prayer to Venus

Of girls till now I'd never tire,
  I fought campaigns not without glory;
Now I'll hang up my arms, and lyre
  That is exhausted by war's story.

They'll grace these side walls that enclose
  The left of Venus of the Sea;
Here, lay bright torches, crowbars, bows,
  That stormed the opposed gates so proudly!

O goddess, Queen of Cyprus fair,
  O Queen of Memphis, where no snowy
Gusts from Sithone fill the air:
  Raise your whip once, and touch proud Chloe!

III.27
To Galatea

The unholy should go on their way
    To the ill-omened barn owl's cry,
The pregnant bitch, the tawny grey
    Wolf that runs down from the high
Country of Lanuvium,
And the vixen great with young.

A slithering snake should, as they ride,
    Break their journey's proposed courses,
Like an arrow from the side,
    Scaring their Gallic coach horses.
I'm a providential seer
For the girl for whom I fear.

Before the bird, which prophesies
    The imminence of violent rain,
On her homeward passage flies,
    Back towards the stagnant fen,
I'll pray for the raven's song
From the coming of the dawn.

May you, wheresoe'er you are,
    Live in true felicity!
Forget me not, Galatea!
    From the left hand of the sky
May no bird prevent you go,
Woodpecker or wandering crow.

Do you see setting Orion,
    With what turbulence he shakes?
I know how the Adriatic can
    Darken, and what a swell it makes,
And how Iapyx from the north west
Seems fair and will then transgress.

May the wives of our enemies
    And their children feel the blind
Motions of the nascent rise
    Of Auster, the fierce southern wind,
And the black ocean's roar and crash,
And coasts shaking beneath the lash.

So, Europa entrusted her side
    Of snowy white to the cunning bull,
And she paled at the teeming tide
    With enormous monsters full;
Caught up in a fraudulent lie,
She blanched at her audacity.

She'd worked among the flowers of late
    In meadow grass, where she could delight
In weaving a garland to dedicate
    To the Nymphs; now, in the glimmering night,
Only the stars in heaven could she
See, and the waves upon the sea.

When to the isle of Crete she came,
  A hundred towns within its sway,
"Father," she cried, "But that's a name
  Your daughter has just given away,
And filial piety and trust
All to raging passion lost!

"I know not whence or whither I came!
  One death alone is a punishment
Too slight for a young virgin's shame!
  Am I awake, as I lament
This foul crime, or, of vices free,
Does an empty ghost play games with me? –

"A ghost that flies through an ivory gate,
  Bringing a dream while I'm asleep!
Ah! Which has been the better fate,
  Over long billows of the deep
To go, or spend those recent hours
Picking bunches of fresh flowers?

"If I were given the infamous bull,
  So much anger do I feel,
I would dedicate my all
  To slash him with a sword of steel
And break the horns of one I loved
So much, but a monster proved.

"Shameless I left my father's house,
    And now shameless I delay
Committing myself to Orcus.
    If any god can hear me say
This prayer, how I wish I could
Wander among lions, nude!

"Before my soft and rounded cheek
    Yields to emaciation foul,
And before the juices leak
    From this young and tender spoil,
I wish, while my looks are good,
I could be the tigers' food!

"My distant father is urging me,
    'Europa, you are worthless trash!
Why do you hesitate to die?
    You can hang from this mountain ash.
Use your girdle to good effect!
Do some damage to your neck!

" 'If you find the cliffs appealing,
    Or the rocks with points of death,
Come and give yourself with feeling
    To the rapid storm wind's breath,
Unless each day you'd rather pluck
A mistress' spinning as your work, –

" 'Though your blood is of royal line, –
Or belong to a foreign dame
And be a paid concubine!'"
As she lamented, Venus came
Smiling falsely at her side,
And her son with bow untied.

The goddess, satisfied with all
Her sport, "You must hold back," said she,
From anger or a fiery brawl,
When, at your time of destiny
The detested bull returns
For you to mutilate his horns.

"You don't know that you are the wife
Of invincible Jove. Now, you must cease
Your sobbing; you must learn in life
To carry great fortune with ease.
A whole continent of the world
Will by your own name be called!"

III.28
To Lyde

What better could I do on the holiday
Of Neptune? Lyde, bring without delay
My treasured Caecuban! Your strength apply
To assault the ramparts of philosophy!

The noonday sun's decline you can now feel,
　　　Yet, as though winged day were standing still,
You hesitate to grab the old wine jar
　　　That since Bibulus' day has been in store.

We'll sing in turns of Neptune and the seas,
　　　And the green tresses of the Nereides;
You'll sing of Lato on your curved lyre
　　　And the sharp darts of speedy Cynthia.

At the song's climax, we will Venus praise,
　　　Queen of Cnidos and the sparkling Cyclades,
Who on yoked swans to Paphos loves to fly;
　　　And then Night in a well-earned lullaby.

III.29
To Maecenas

Son of Etruscan kings of yore,
　　　Smooth wine from flasks I've yet to pour,
Maenenas, and the rose's flower
　　　And oil of ben pressed for your hair

Wait at my house. Quick, no delay!
　　　Don't watch damp Tibur and Aefula
With sloping fields, and the mountainside
　　　Of Telegonus the parricide.

Give up tiresome prosperity,
　　　Your mansion climbing to the sky!
Don't stare at the city smoke and gaze
　　　At blessed Rome's wealth and noisy ways!

Often, the rich find change welcome;
　　　Within a poor man's tiny home
No purple drapes, but tidy fare
　　　Will smooth away the frown of care.

Andromeda's bright father shows
　　　His secret fire; and mad Leo's
Constellation and Procyon
　　　Rage, as the sun brings dry days on.

Tired shepherds with their languid flocks
　　　Seek shade and stream, and the thorny copse
Of rough Silvan; mute rivers find
　　　No respite from the wandering wind.

You care what stance will most become
　　　The state; anxious you fear for Rome
The plots of feuding Tanais,
　　　And Cyrus' realm, and the Chinese.

The future's outcome with foresight
　　　God hides in the dark mists of night;
If mortals fuss more than they may,
　　　He laughs. Remember, plan today

With a tranquil mind! The rest is borne
        As if by a river slipping down
Its central channel peacefully
        Out into the Etruscan sea,

But then it rolls up polished stones,
        Uprooted trees and herds and homes;
The mountains and the neighbouring woods
        All rage and shout, as the wild floods

Harass the quiet streams. He'll be
        His own master and live happily,
Who day to day can say out loud,
        "I've lived! Tomorrow, with black cloud

Or pure sun let God fill the sky:
        He'll not make void what has passed by,
Reshape or render it undone,
        When once the fleeting hour has gone."

Fortune enjoys her savage work;
        From her strange game she does not shirk;
Uncertain honours she'll transmute;
        To me, then to others, she is good.

I praise her when she stays, but if
        She flaps her wings, gifts back I give;
I wrap myself in my own worth
        And, undowried, woo honest dearth.

It's not for me, if the mainmast roars
    In an African storm, to have recourse
To bargains, vows and piteous prayers
    That Cyprian and Tyrian wares

Shan't add my wealth to the grasping sea!
    Safely, in a two-oared dinghy,
Through the Aegean hurricanes,
    I'll sail by the breezes and the Twins.

III.30
Epilogue

I've made a monument to outlast bronze,
Rise higher than the pyramid of a king;
No gnawing rain, no north wind's violence,
Or countless ranks of years and the fleeing
Of time could e'er this monument erase.
I shall not all die; some great part of me
Will escape Death's goddess. With posthumous praise,
I'll freshly grow, be renewed constantly,
So long as priest with silent priestess shall
Climb upward to the Roman Capitol.
I shall be famed where Aufidus' torrents roar
And where waterless Daunus reigned as king
Of rustic folk. Humble, I rose to power,
And I became the first of men to sing
Aeolian song transposed to Italian measures.
Let my merits afford you supreme pleasures:
Grant me the Delphic laurel willingly,
And crown my head with it, Melpomene.

Book IV

IV.1

To Venus

Venus, are you resuming war
   After so long? Spare me, I implore!
I am not the same today
   As when good Cinara held sway.
O sweet Cupids' mother wild,
   Don't bend me with your dictates mild,
Hardened after fifty years!
   Go, heed young men's flattering prayers!
You had better fly at once
   On the wings of purple swans
And hurry to Paullus' home,
   Where your fever can consume
A ready heart; for he's well born,
   Decent and no taciturn
Advocate of tough defences,
   With a hundred competences.
Far and wide the boy will carry
   The colours of your military
And, when he has won success
   And laughed at his rival's largesse,
He'll see your marble statue gleams
   By the Alban lake beneath citrus beams.
You'll smell incense, enjoy the lute,
   Hear the Berecyntian flute,
And the pipe will play along
   With a miscellany of song.
Boys and young girls twice each day
   Will there extol your deity;

Salian style, with pure white feet,
  They'll shake the ground with triple beat.
For me, no lady love or boy
  Or credulous hope of mutual joy,
No drinking bout helps pass the hours,
  Nor crowning my head with fresh flowers.
But why, – oh, Ligurinus, speak! –
  Does a sole tear slip down my cheek,
And my tongue, mid my eloquence,
  Lapse into unseemly silence?
At night I dream I hold you tight
  Or follow you when you're in flight
Across the Field of Mars or through
  The rolling waters, cruel you!

IV.2
To Iullus

Whoever, Iullus, strives to emulate
Pindar, reaches with Daedalus for the sky
On waxen wings and is destined to donate
  His name to the glassy sea.

Just as a mountain river downward flows,
When heavy rains have fed it far beyond
Its usual banks, Pindar boils, falls and grows
  Massive, with a voice profound.

How he deserves Apollo's crown of bay!
In audacious dithyrambic refrain
He rolls down new words and is borne away
    On rhythms no laws constrain,

Or he sings songs of gods, kings and gods' blood,
Those at whose hands the Centaurs rightly came
To their last fall, and others who subdued
    Fearful Chimaera's flame.

Of horse and boxer coming home once more,
Exalted by the Olympic palm to the skies,
He tells, giving a prize of greater power
    Than a hundred effigies.

He mourns the youth snatched from his weeping love,
Praising his manly strength, his mental spark
And golden virtues to the stars above,
    Denying Orcus dark.

A mass of air lifts this swan of Dirce
Whenever he climbs up to the high tracts
Of the clouds. I, I am like a Matine bee
    In my ways and my acts,

Who gathers sweet thyme with unceasing toil,
Working around the woodland and along
The banks of wet Tibur: a creature small,
    I shape my busy song.

You'll sing, Iullus, with a more grand plectrum,
Of Caesar, when he up the Sacred Way

Dragging the fierce Sygambrians shall come,
    Crowned with triumphal bay,

Than whom no greater and no better thing
Have Fates and good gods given to the world,
Nor will they give, even at a new coming
    Of the former age of gold.

You'll sing, also, of joyous days in Rome
And public games on the return hard sought
Of valiant Augustus to his home,
    And the empty law court.

Then, if I, too, can say words fit to hear,
My voice will also bear its own good part:
At Caesar's welcome, "Praise to the Sun so fair!"
    I'll sing with a happy heart.

Not once, but three times, we will shout the words
"Joy! Triumph!" as you go. The whole city
Will cry, and we'll burn incense to the gods
    For their generosity.

Ten bulls and ten cows will absolve your vows;
A young bull calf which in thick grasses feeds,
Abandoned by its mother as it grows,
    Will meet my promised needs.

The curved fires of the crescent moon, that light
At her third rising, will grace his forehead;
Where he is branded, he will be snow white,
    Elsewhere a tawny red.

IV.3
To Melpomene

He, whom at birth with kindly eye
   You've once looked on, Melpomene,
Will never rise to boxing fame
   Through hard work at an Isthmian game;
No keen horse with Achaean car
   Will bring him victory; no war
Will put him on the Capitol stage
   Adorned with Delian foliage
For crushing some king's trumped up force!
   But streams that past rich Tibur course
And woodlands with leaves thick and strong
   Ennoble him with Aeolian song.
O Rome, of cities the princess,
   Now envy's tooth will gnaw me less;
Your children have set me on high
   In their beloved poets' company.
Pierian Muse, you who instill
   Sweet sounds in the gold tortoiseshell,
Who even to the speechless fish
   Will give a swan's voice if you wish,
This is all due to your bounty,
   That passers-by now point at me,
The minstrel of the Roman lyre, –
   I breathe and please, but you inspire!

IV.4
In Praise of Drusus

Like the winged servant of the thunderbolt,
    Whom Jove made king of the birds' roving breed,
Himself the king of gods, when without fault
    The eagle helped him win fair Ganymede:

Youthfulness and his forebears' energy
    Drove the bird out unpractised from his nest,
And then spring winds, sweeping the clouds away,
    Taught him to put new efforts to the test,

Though fearful; soon, in spirited attack
    He dives upon sheep pens in hostile flight
Or falls on serpents as they wrestle back, –
    He's so in love with feasting and the fight, –

Or like a lion that his mother shakes
    Off from the rich milk of her tawny side, –
A deer intent on happy grazing wakes
    To perish by a tooth till now untried.

And so, beneath the Alps, as he made war,
    Was Drusus by the Vindelici seen,
Who throughout history by tradition bore
    Their Amazonian battleaxes keen.

Whence came this custom need not be revealed –
    To know all things is not right! – but, though long
And far and wide they vanquished in the field,
    They were revanquished by plans of the young.

They felt the power of sound intelligence
    And talent raised in an auspicious home,
And of Augustus' fatherly presence
    Toward boys who from Nero's stock had come.

The brave are made so by the brave and good;
    The colt and young bull in their own selves prove
Their fathers' courage; and the eagle's blood
    Does not beget the soft unwarlike dove.

But teaching builds upon inherent force
    And proper training fortifies the breast;
When morals follow a defective course,
    The well-born is by ugly guilt possessed.

How much, Rome, to the Neros' clan you owe,
    River Metaurus, Hasdrubal's defeat,
And that fine day do all bear witness to,
    When Latium's dark to lightness made retreat.

In bounteous glory then, day smiled, the first
    Since the African through towns of Italy,
A flame through pine trees, rode his ride accursed,
    Like Eurus on the waves of Sicily.

Then, Rome's young manhood knew success, and toiled
    And grew, restoring every holy shrine
That impious Carthaginians had despoiled
    With upright statues of the gods divine.

At length, perfidious Hannibal declared,
    "We're deer! We are the rapacious wolf's prey!
Perversely we pursue, when our reward
    Is more if we escape and run away!

"This race, which bravely from cremated Troy
    Brought holy relics tossed on Tuscan seas,
And carried aged father and small boy
    Across to the Ausonian cities,

"Is like a great oak pruned by axes hard
    On Algidus abounding with dark leaves;
Through loss, through carnage, from the very sword,
    Fresh spirit and resources it receives.

"The Hydra was not sturdier when it grew
    Its shorn leaves to frustrate fierce Hercules;
No greater monster Colchis ever knew,
    Or dragon Echion's city of Thebes.

"Submerge them in the deep, they emerge more fair;
    Wrestle, and with true credit they rush out
Against their undefeated conqueror
    In battles for their wives to talk about!

"No longer now to Carthage shall I send
    Proud messengers. Destroyed are our hopes all!
And our name's destiny has reached its end
    With the destruction of great Hasdrubal."

So Claudian hands have perfect competence;
    Jove's benign presence keeps them safe and sure,
And Claudian intellect and diligence
    Haste them through the emergencies of war.

IV.5
To Augustus Caesar

Born of the good gods, guardian excellent
    Of Romulus' race, and far too long absent:
Within the sacred council you did swear
    To Rome's fathers a timely return here.

Come back, good prince! Give back your land your light!
    When, like the spring, your countenance glows bright
Upon the nation, then more pleasant run
    The days and more intensely shines the sun.

And when the south wind comes, and selfishly
    Blows on the wastes of the Carpathian Sea,
Keeping a young man lingering on the foam
    For more than one year, far from his sweet home –

His mother with vows, pleas and tokens, prays
    And never takes her eyes off the curved bays! –
So, Romans, too, with loyal longing yearn
    That Caesar to his country should return.

The ox in safety roams the countryside
That Ceres feeds, good Fortune at her side;
And sailors across peaceful waters fly,
And censure is abhorred by honesty.

The pure house is by no defilement stained;
By law and usage tainted sin is tamed;
Babies' familial looks win compliments;
Crime is suppressed by fitting punishments.

With Caesar unharmed, who could ever fear
Parthians or foes from icy Scythia,
Or broods that the rough German nation bore;
Or worry at fierce Iberia and her war?

Each man on his own hillside spends his days
And weds the vine to the unmarried trees;
Thence to his wines he goes home in glad mood,
Inviting you to his main course as god!

He honours you with fulsome prayer and wine
From his libation bowls; Caesar divine
He mixes with household divinities,
As Greece lauds both Castor and Hercules.

"Good prince, grant Italy a long holiday,"
In early morning soberly we say,
When day is whole and fresh, and say it drunk
After the sun has under Ocean sunk.

IV.6
Hymn to Apollo

O god, your vengeance at their massive boast
    Niobe's children felt; and Tityos fell,
The rapist, and Achilles who almost
    Won victory o'er Troy's lofty citadel,

The Phthian warrior, greater than them all,
    But not your equal, though son of Marine
Thetis, and though he shook the towers and wall
    Of Ilium with his awesome javelin.

Like a great pine tree axed by biting steel,
    Or cypress that the north wind's blast might wreck,
With his giant frame outspread he prostrate fell
    And in the Trojan dust laid down his neck.

He'd not have wished to hide within the horse
    That feigned Minerva's sacred offering,
Or dupe the Trojans in their revels' course,
    Or Priam's palace joyful with dancing,

But would have planned in sin vengeance to wreak
    And, as his captives watched, – alas! – consume
With Grecian flames boys who did not yet speak,
    Even the child within its mother's womb,

Unless the Father of the Gods had given,
    Swayed by your voice and by dear Venus' prayers,
Walls built beneath a more auspicious heaven,
    To save Aeneas' race in future years.

Minstrel, teacher of clear voiced Thalia,
     Washing your hair where River Xanthus flows,
Smooth-faced Apollo, guard from failure
     Our Daunian Camena, Italy's Muse!

Phoebus has given me his inspiration,
     Phoebus the art of song, a poet's name:
O girls who are the first girls of the nation,
     And boys who come from fathers of fair fame,

Wards of Delos' goddess, to whose bow fleeting
     Lynxes and antelopes meekly succumb,
Keep to the Sapphic metre and the beating –
     Observe the rhythmic beating of my thumb!

Now duly praise Latona's youthful son!
     Praise the Night-Shiner with her rising light,
Who feeds the crops and makes the steep months run,
     Rolling them swiftly on in downward flight.

When you are wed, you'll say, "For the gods above,
     When the new century brought festive days,
I once performed a song that they might love,
     And learned the music of the bard Horace!"

IV.7
To Torquatus

The snows have scattered; now upon the leas
      The grass returns, and leaves upon the trees;
Earth changes seasons and the floods subside;
      Again within their banks the rivers glide.

Now the three Graces and the Nymphs advance
      And venture out unclothed to lead the dance.
The year and the hour that steals indulgent day
      Warn to hope not for immortality.

The winter's cold is warmed by the west wind,
      And spring gives way to summer, which must end
Once fruitful autumn has poured forth its store,
      And then still winter hurries back once more.

The moons in their swift courses soon repair
      The heaven's damage, but when we fall there,
Where pious Aeneas and wealthy Tullus
      And Ancus fell, we are shadow and dust.

Who knows whether the gods in their high home
      Will add tomorrow's times to today's sum?
But gifts, which to your own dear heart you make,
      Your heir with grasping hands can never take.

Once you have perished and your destiny
      Is fixed by Minos with his clear decree,
No eloquence, nobility of birth
      Or piety will bring you back to earth.

From nether gloom Diana cannot free
    Hippolytus, for all his chastity;
By Lethe's streams Pirithous remains,
    For Theseus is too weak to break his chains.

IV.8
To Censorinus

I'd willingly give bowls and gifts of bronze
To all my good friends and companions;
I would give tripods, prizes that the brave
Greeks win, – the very best of these you'd have,
If only I were rich in works of art
That Scopas and Parrhasius create;
For one in marble, one with colours could
Produce the likeness of a man or god.
But this is not my strength and these are toys
That you don't need by circumstance or choice.
You enjoy songs, and songs I can create;
A price for this gift I will even state!
No marble statue inscribed with public praise,
By which the spirit and their former days
Return to dead princes, nor the retreat
In haste of Hannibal, nor any threat
Flung back at him, nor impious Carthage's fire
Lit by him, who in saving Africa,
Received its surname, more clearly declare
Men's praise than Muses from Calabria;
And if the writing paper does not say
What good you've done, you won't have had your pay!
What would become of Troy's and Mars's son,

If silence, envious and taciturn,
Prevented the just fame of Romulus?
From River Styx was rescued Aeacus,
Whom virtue, popularity and the tongue
Of greater poets consecrates among
The blessed isles. The Muse will not let die
The praiseworthy, but lauds them to the sky.
So doughty Hercules is asked as guest
By Jupiter to attend his choicest feast,
And the bright stars of Castor and Pollux keep
Men's storm-tossed ships from waters of the deep,
And with green vine-shoots garlanding his brow
Liber brings good results to mortal vow.

IV.9
To Lollius

Lest you may think my words will die,
    Which by arts ne'er divulged before,
Born by resonant Aufidus, I
    Join to the chords of my guitar,

Though Homer takes the highest place
    To ignore Pindar would be wrong,
Or Stesichorus' serious lays,
    Alcaeus' menace and Cean song.

Anacreon's eternal wit
    Age has not dulled; and love still breathes,
And passion with its vital heat
    On Sappho's Lesbian lyre-strings seethes.

Helen was not the only wife
    On fire for gold clothes, coiffured hair,
The princely friends and royal life
    Of an admired adulterer,

Teucer not first with Cretan bow
    To shoot arrows; not once did war
Vex Troy, nor only huge Greeks go
    Where other men had gone before,

To battles fit for the Muses' voice;
    Fierce Hector and Deiphobus keen,
For modest wives and their young boys,
    Were not the first of heroes slain.

Before Agamemnon brave men lived,
    Many; all weighed down by long night,
But, of a holy bard deprived,
    Unwept with unreported plight.

Virtue concealed is short remove
    From buried idleness, but I
Will on my page your honour prove,
    Nor suffer with impunity

Your many labours to collect
    A bruised crop of forgetfulness.
Your mind is prudent and correct,
    In good times and when under stress,

Resolved to punish greed and fraud,
      Avoiding all-amassing wealth,
Consul not for a year's reward,
      But for as long as trust and health

Set honesty ahead of gain,
      And with high head rejecting bribes,
And vanquishing with might and main
      Through all the opposition's tribes.

The rich man you'd not truly call
      Blessed; more properly he gets
The name of blessed for using all
      God's bounties for wise benefits.

He can endure hard poverty,
      And fears disgrace more than life's end;
He is no coward afraid to die
      For his country or a dear friend.

IV.10

To Ligurinus

Still you are cruel, although the gifts of love
Through Venus' potency you could provide;
But soon the beard of manhood will remove,
Against your hopes, all of your boyhood's pride.
Your hair, which now upon your shoulder flows,
Will lose its substance and will fall away;
Your colour, now more lovely than a rose
Abloom with scarlet blossoms, will decay.
Then, when your beard bristles, you'll cry "Alas!"
Mourning the altered aspect you employ,
Whenever you peer in the looking-glass:
"Why had I not today's mind as a boy?
          And why, when I these new attentions seek,
          Does former purity not grace my cheek?"

IV.11

To Phyllis

I've a full flask of Alban wine,
        Phyllis, that's nine years old and more;
My garden has parsley you can twine
        For garlands, and a mighty store

Of ivy to bind your shining hair.
        The silver smiles within my home;
Chaste vervain covers my old altar
        That craves the sacrifice of a lamb.

Hither and thither servants hurry;
        The slave boys run, the busy girls;
And rolling flames flicker and carry
        Black smoke that up the chimney curls.

Please understand this joyful date!
        You're called to keep the Ides with me,
Which April's mid-point celebrate,
        The month of Venus of the Sea.

This truly is a solemn day,
        Almost more sacred, it appears,
Than my own birthday; from today
        Maecenas counts his flowing years!

Telephus, whom you like to chase,
        Is not a lad that you can gain;
He's owned by a rich, playful lass,
        Who keeps him on a pleasant chain.

Phaethon's scorching by Jove's fire
    Scares off high hopes; the winged flight
Of Pegasus sets an example dire,
    For he threw off his earthly knight,

Bellerophon. Keep to what is fit!
    Do not unequal loves approve!
Don't hope beyond the right limit!
    Come to me now, my own last love, –

No other girl will keep me warm, –
    Learn, learn the music! Come along,
And with your lovely voice perform!
    Dark cares will become less with song.

IV.12
To Virgil

Now spring's companions who calm the sea,
    The Thracian breezes into the sails blow,
    And now no pastures freeze, not winter snow
Swells rivers roaring in cacophony.

The unhappy swallow builds her nest and sings,
    Weeping for Itys and the eternal shame
    Of Cecrops' house, because with evil name
She avenged the barbaric lustfulness of kings.

Now, to the pipe, guardians of fat sheep play
       Their songs upon the fresh and tender sward,
       And so they charm the god, who loves the herd
And the dark hillsides of Arcadia.

This season brings on thirst, my dear Virgil!
       If wine that's pressed at Cales is your plan, –
       And you the client of young noblemen, –
You'll need some nard to pay for your wine bill.

A little onyx tub of nard will buy
       A flask that now lies in Sulpicius' store,
       To give new hopes in generous measure, or
To wash the bitter taste of cares away.

If you're keen for these pleasures, quickly come
       With your own merchandise! It's not my intent
       To soak you in my cups without payment,
As though a rich man with a well stocked home.

But put aside delays and thoughts of gain!
       Remember, while you may, death's darker fire,
       And high thoughts with brief foolishness inspire!
It's sweet at times to have a fuddled brain.

IV.13
To Lyce

The gods have heard my prayers; you're getting old.
　　The gods have heard, and still, Lyce, Lyce,
You want to seem a beauty to behold:
　　You frolic and you drink immoderately,

And in your cups with tremulous song you seek
　　To rouse slow Cupid. But he's out on guard
Upon the girl from Chios' lovely cheek;
　　And she's in bloom and good at the guitar!

Disdainfully, he flies past withered oaks;
　　He shrinks from you because, it must be said,
Your stained and yellow teeth debase your looks,
　　Those wrinkles and the snow upon your head.

No robes of Coan purple now remain;
　　No precious stones recall the times you passed,
Forever filed in the public domain
　　Where winged day has imprisoned them at last.

Where are your lover's charms, the way you moved,
　　The colour of your skin? Where did they flee?
What's left of her, of her who breathed and loved,
　　And with her love stole my own self from me?

Happy and honoured after Cinara,
　　You were the epitome of gracious arts;
But fate gave just a few brief years to her,
　　And yet to you a long life it imparts.

You'll be a small old crow, my dear Lýce,
  And lusty lads will send you on your way
With many a laugh, because they'll clearly see
  A burnt out torch to ash faded away.

IV.14
To Augustus Caesar

How will the Senate and People of Rome
  Perpetuate, Augustus, and record
Through texts and inscriptions for years to come
  Your virtue with fair honour's full reward,

Where'er the sun lights habitable shores,
  Greatest of all princes, Rome's emperor?
From you rough Vindelici learned the laws
  Of Latium and your potency in war.

For with your forces Drusus more than once
  Threw down the Genaunians' impatient race
And swift Breuni; from towering Alpine mounts
  He hurled their castles down with eager face.

Soon, the older Nero commenced battle grave
  And drove the monstrous Raeti from the field;
To him the sky auspicious omens gave;
  His glory in Mars' contest was revealed.

Then to what great destruction he consigned
    Hearts that were sworn to death and liberty,
Almost like Auster's turbulent south wind
    That stirs the untamed waves upon the sea,

When the fair chorus of the Pleiades
    Breaks through the clouds! So quick was he, indeed,
To vex the squadrons of his enemies
    And through the fire's heart ride his neighing steed.

As rolling bull-shaped Aufidus appears,
    That past Apulian Daunus' kingdom flows,
When he goes wild and fearful floods prepares
    To devastate the tilled fields and meadows,

So, at his vast assault on foreign foe,
    The ironclad columns fell to Claudius;
Their first and then their last down he did mow,
    Strewing the ground, a victor without loss.

But you, Augustus, did the troops provide,
    The strategy and your gods. For on the date
When suppliant Alexandria opened wide
    Her ports and her deserted palace gate,

Propitious Fortune, after fifteen years,
    Gave to your wars a favourable end,
And brought the praise and glory Rome desires
    On the accomplishment of your command.

You, the Cantabrian untamed before,
	Mede, Indian and Scythian in flight,
You, all these nations worship and adore,
	Guardian of Italy and Roman might;

You, Nile who hides the sources of his springs,
	You, Hister and Tigris that swiftly runs,
You, Ocean hears, teeming with monstrous things
	And crashing on the far removed Britons;

You, Gaul's land that no funerals affright,
	You, the earth of hard Iberia obeys;
Sygambri who in massacre delight
	Lay down their arms and sing you songs of praise.

IV.15
The Augustan Age

When Phoebus saw I wished to tell the tale
	Of battles and of foreign victories,
He beat his lyre and warned me not to sail
	With my small rig across the Tuscan seas.

The Augustan Age our rich crops reinstates
	And to Rome's God our standards now restores
Torn down from Parthia's haughty temple gates;
	The age has closed Janus's warless doors.

The licence, which can strict rules override,
      Has been curbed by restrictions and commands;
This age has pushed both guilt and crime aside,
      And ancient arts and skills it now demands.

Through these the Latin name and Italy's strength
      Have grown, her fame and empire's majesty,
Which to the eastern sun stretches its length
      From the sun's couch beneath the western sea.

With Caesar as our institutions' guard,
      No civil rage or force will drive out peace;
Nor yet the ire that hammers out the sword
      And brings hostilities to sad cities.

No drinkers of the Danube's waters deep
      Will break your Julian edicts, nor Chinese,
Getans or Persians who no trust can keep,
      Nor men raised near the River Tanais.

Surrounded by the bounties Liber gives,
      We, both on common and on holy day,
Together with our children and our wives,
      After we first to heaven with due rites pray,

We'll sing our princes' glorious attributes
      As in the past our forefathers have done, –
In song accompanied by Lydian flutes, –
      And Troy, Anchises and kind Venus' son.

Carmen Saeculare

Phoebus and mighty Diana holding sway
Over the forests, heaven's bright ornament,
Worshipped and worshipful, to our prayers consent
    On this holy day.

The Sibylline verses have bidden at this time
Selected maidens and innocent boys
To address the gods, who in seven hills rejoice,
    With a new hymn.

Bountiful Sun, you who with shining car
Draw out the day and hide it, born anew
And yet the same, may nothing that you view
    Exceed Rome's power.

And you, who open the ripened womb aright,
Be gentle, be the mothers' protectress,
Whose name is Life-Giver, our birth goddess,
    And Giver of Light.

Bring forth our offspring, prosper the decrees
Our fathers gave concerning intercourse
For womankind and matrimonial laws
    For fruitful increase,

So the sure cycle of eleven times ten full years
Will bring hymns and the rush of games again,
Three times when day is bright and thrice more when
    Cool night appears.

You Fates, who in song and perfect truth declare
What's once been said and what the bounds fixed fast
Of history shall secure, join to our past
   A destiny fair.

May Earth, abundant in her herds and fruits,
Give garlands of her corn unto Ceres,
And may Jove's wholesome waters and his breeze
   Nourish the broods.

Mildly and peacefully lay down your spear,
Apollo! Harken to our suppliant boys!
Moon, horned Queen of Stars, attend the voice
   Of our girls! Hear!

Rome is your work and your creation, yours,
Since Trojan squadrons held the Etruscan strand,
Commanded to change household gods and land
   On a safe course.

Through Ilium's guiltless fire Aeneas chaste,
Destined for them his fatherland to survive,
Protected their free passage, so to give
   More than they lost.

Gods, grant to ready youth true probity!
Gods, peaceful rest to quiet old age donate!
To Romulus' race give progeny, estate,
   All dignity!

You, whom with snow-white bulls we venerate,
We, Venus' and Anchises' glorious blood,

Make us supreme in war, but make us good
    To foes prostrate!

The Medes and Persians fear our powerful hands
And Alban axes on both land and seas,
And once-proud Scythians now sue for peace
    And Indians.

Now Faith, Peace, Honour, ancient Modesty
And Manliness neglected dare return,
And blessed Plenty's overbrimming horn
    Gladdens the eye.

Prophetic Phoebus decked with shining bow,
Beloved and welcomed by the Muses nine,
Raising to health the weary limbs of men,
    Skilled Apollo,

May he with grace look on the Palatine,
May he prolong the Commonwealth of Rome
And happy Latium for a further term
    And age more fine!

May she of the Aventine and Algidus,
Diana, hearken to the Fifteen Men,
And may she attend the prayers of our children
    With kindly ears!

That Jove and all the gods may feel the same,
I take back home a hope that's strong and sure,
Trained to praise Phoebus as a chorister
    And Diana's name.

Appendix I

Horace: Ode to Phyllis
Latin text

Est mihi nonum superantis annum
plenus Albani cadus; est in horto,
Phylli, nectendis apium coronis;
  est hederae vis

multa, qua crines religata fulges;
ridet argento domus; ara castis
vincta verbenis avet immolato
  spargier agno;

cuncta festinat manus, huc et illuc
cursitant mixtae pueris puellae;
sordidum flammae trepidant rotantes
  vertice fumum.

ut tamen noris quibus advoceris
gaudiis, Idus tibi sunt agendae,
qui dies mensem Veneris marinae
  findit Aprilem,

iure sollemnis mihi sanctiorque
paene natali proprio, quod ex hac
luce Maecenas meus adfluentis
  ordinat annos.

Telephum, quem tu petis, occupavit
non tuae sortis iuvenem puella
dives et lasciva tenetque grata
  compede vinctum.

terret ambustus Phaethon avaras
spes, et exemplum grave praebet ales
Pegasus terrenum equitem gravatus
  Bellerophontem,

semper ut te digna sequare et ultra
quam licet sperare nefas putando
disparem vites. age iam, meorum
  finis amorum —

non enim posthac alia calebo
femina — condisce modos, amanda
voce quos reddas: minuentur atrae
  carmine curae.

Appendix II

Musical Interpretation: M425 Ode to Phyllis

The first part of this appendix interprets the M425 neumes on the assumption that the second stanza begins on middle C. The text is hyphenated to show how it relates musically to the neumes. M425 has no musical notation for the last three stanzas of the ode.

? ? ? ?   *DD C D - - -*
Est mihi nonum   *superantis annum*

? ? ? D E-CD   *F ? A G F-F D*
plenus Alba-ani   *cadus; est in ho-orto,*

G-A-G E FG-G D   *AGAFG-AA*
Phy-y-ylli, necte-endis   *apium coro-onis;*

G-A DCE-E D
e-est hedera-ae vis

C D F D-ED   *DDCD EE*
multa, qua cri-ines   *religata fulges;*

E-G E D E-CD   *F G AG F-F D*
r i-i det arge-ento   *domus; ara ca-astis*

G-A-GEFG-GD   *AG AF G-AA*
vi-i-incta verbe-enis   *avet immola-ato*

G-A DCE-E D
spa-argier a-agno;

C DFD-ED
cuncta festi-inat

D D CD EE
manus, huc et illuc

E-G E D E-CD
cu-ursitant mi-ixtae

F G A GF-FD
pueris   pue-ellae;

G-A-GE F G-G   D
So---ordidum fla-ammae

[*AG*] A FG-AA
trepidant rota-antes

G-ADCE-E D
ve-ertice fu-umum.

C D[F] D-ED
ut tamen no-oris

D D C DEE
quibus advoceris

E-GED E-CD
ga-udiis, I-idus

F G A   GF-F D
tibi sunt   age-endae,

G-A-GEF G-G D
qui-i-i dies me-ensem

A G A FG-AA
Veneris mari-inae

G-AD C E-ED
fi-indit Apri-ilem,

C D FD-E D
iure   solle-emnis

DD C DE E
mihi sanctiorque

E-GE DE-CD
pa-aene nata-ali

F GA F-GF-F D
proprio, quo-od e-ex hac

G-*A*-*GEF G*-*GD*

lu-u-uce Maece-enas

A *G AFG*-*AA*

meus adflue-entis

G-*ADC E*-*E D*

o-ordinat a-annos.

C *D F D D*

Telephum, quem tu

D *D CDEE*

petis, occupavit

E-*G ED E*-*CD*

no-on tuae so-ortis

F *G A GF*-*FD*

iuvenem pue-ella

G-*A*-*GEFGG*-*GD*

di-i-i-ves et lasci-iv-a

A*G*-*A F G*-*AA*

tene-etque gra-ata

G-*A DC E*-*E D*

co-ompede vi-inctum.

The following part of this appendix takes the musical interpretation forward on a treble clef in 3:4 time. I am indebted to Iain Kerr for his help in this project.

Musical Interpretation: M425 Ode to Phyllis
(Lyons and Kerr)

1. Est mihi no......num super-an- tis an- num
2. mul- ta qua cri-..... nes re-li- ga- ta ful- ges;
3. cunc-ta fes- ti-.........nat manus, huc et il- luc
4. ut tamen no-.......ris quibus ad- vo- ce- ris
5. iu- re sol- lem-....nis mihi sanc- ti- or- que
6. Tel- ephum quem tu petis oc- cu- pa- vit
7. ter- ret am- bus-....tus Pha-e-thon a- va- ras
8. sem- per ut te dig- na sequar(e) et ult- ra
9. non enim post- hac a- li- a ca- le- bo

1. ple-....nus Al- ba-.........ni cadus; est in hor-.....to
2. ri-....det ar- gen-......to domus; a- ra cas-.....tis
3. cur-....sitant mix-.....tae puer- is pu- el-......lae
4. gau-...di- is, I-........dus tibi sunt a- gen-....dae,
5. pae-....ne na- ta-........li *see Note 1 below*
6. no-.....n tu- ae sor-......tis iuve- nem pu- el-.......la
7. spe.....s et ex- em-.....plum grave praebet a-........les
8. qua-...m licet spe-......ra- re ne- fas pu tan-.....do
9. fe-........mina – con-....dis- ce mo- dos, a- man- da

1. Phyl-…li, nec- ten-……dis api- um co- ro-……nis
2. vinc-…ta ver- be-………nis avet im- mo- la-…….tum
3. sor-….di- dum flam-……mae trepidant ro- tan-…….tes
4. qui…..di- es men-…….sem Veneris ma- ri-……….nae
5. lu-…….ce Mae- ce-……….as meus ad- flu-en-……..tes
6. *see Note 2 below*
7. Pe-…..ga- sus ter-….ren(um) equitem gra-va-……tus
8. dis-….par-em vi-………tes. age iam, me-o-……..rum
9. vo-…..ce quos red-…….das: minuen- tur at-…….rae

1. e-…st he-de- rae……vis
2. spar-… gier ag-……..no;
3. ver-… tice fu-……mum.
4. fin-…. dit Ap-ri-…….lem
5 or-…. dinat an-……nos.
6. com-……pede vinc-…..tum.
7. Bel-……..lero- phon-….tem
8. fi-……….nis a- mo-……rum –
9. car-……..mine cu-………rae

Note 1:

In stanza 5, line 2, the second half-line emphasises the word *quod* (because) and the music reads:

propri-o, qu- od e-....x hac

Note 2:

In stanza 6, line 3, the musical treatment of the weak caesura emphasises the word *lasciva* (playful, sexy) and suggests a humerous rallentando before the music picks up again. The music reads:

di-.....ves et   las- ci.........va   tene-..tque gra-........ta

The musical interpretation in all the staves above is the intellectual property of the author and his musical collaborator.

Appendix III

Ut queant laxis
Paul the Deacon: Verses in Praise of St John the Baptist
Latin Text and English Verse Translation

Ut queant laxis resonare fibris
mira gestorum famuli tuorum,
solve polluti labii reatum,
sancte Iohannes!

Nuntius celso veniens Olympo
te patri magnum fore nasciturum,
nomen et vitae seriem gerendae
ordine promit.

Ille promissi dubius superni
perdidit promptae modulos loquelae;
sed reformasti genitus peremptae
organa vocis.

Ventris abstruso positus cubili
senseras regem thalamo manentem,
hinc parens nati meritis uterque
abdita pandit.

Antra deserti teneris sub annis
civium turmas fugiens, petisti,
ne levi saltim maculare vitam
famine posses.

Praebuit hirtum tegimen camelus,
artubus sacris strofium bidentis,
cui latex haustum, sociata pastum
    mella locustis.

Caeteri tantum cecinere vatum
corde praesago iubar adfuturum;
tu quidem mundi scelus auferentem
    indice prodis.

Non fuit vasti spatium per orbis
sanctior quisquam genitus Iohanne,
qui nefas saecli meruit lavantem
    tingere limphis.

O nimis felix meritique celsi
nesciens labem nivei pudoris,
prepotens martyr heremique culto,
    maxime vatum!

Serta ter denis alios coronant
aucta crementis, duplicate quosdam;
trina centeno cumulate fructu
    te, sacer, ornant.

Nunc potens nostri meritis opimis
pectoris duros lapides repelle
asperum planans iter, et reflexos
    dirige calles,

ut pius mundi sator et redemptor
mentibus pulsa luvione puris
rite dignetur veniens sacratos
    ponere gressus.

Laudibus cives celebrant superni
te, dues simplex, pariterque trine,
supplices ac nos veniam precamur:
parce redemptis!

Hymn to St John the Baptist: English Version

O free our sinful lips from stain
    That we your servants may rejoice
At your great miracles again,
    Holy St John, with open voice!

A messenger from heaven came
    To tell of your portentous birth
And to reveal your deeds and name,
    And all your lifetime's future worth.

Doubting the promise from on high,
    Your father lost both speech and word;
But at your birth you graciously
    His vocal instrument restored.

Within the deep bed of the womb
    A royal presence on you pressed;

Each parent of a child to come
　　His secret merits then expressed.
In desert caves your youth you spent,
　　Fleeing the city-dwellers' strife
And fearing hunger might present
　　Temptation for your perfect life.

A camel gave you its rough shade,
　　Your holy chaplet from a beast;
You drank its milk and your meal made;
　　Honey and locust were your feast.

O joyous saint of merit high
　　Whose modesty is pure as snow,
Great martyr sent to prophesy
　　And live a hermit here below!

Some saints claim thirty woven crowns
　　With increase fair, some twice three tens;
Your holiness three hundred owns,
　　Laden with fruitful sustenance.

Save us for gainful purpose now,
　　Cast off the hard stones from our heart,
Smooth our rough journey as we go,
　　Make straight our paths as we depart,

That the creator of mankind,
　　Pious redeemer of our dearth,
May banish sin and cleanse our mind,
　　His hallowed steps upon the earth.

The heavenly hosts praise you alway,
You two in one and one in three,
And suppliants we for pardon pray:
Redeem and spare us with mercy!

Note:
Guido d'Arezzo used the Horatian melody for the first stanza only
of Paul the Deacon's Latin. There is no evidence of the musical
setting being used for the verse composition as a whole.

Bibliography

Primary Sources

Horace
Fontes Iuris Romani Anteiustiniani I.40
Corpus Inscriptionum Latinarum VI.32323 (ILS 5050)
M425 Codex of Horace
Vatican Reg Lat 1672 and 1703

Appian	Civil Wars
Aristophanes	Knights
Dio Cassius	Roman History; Reign of Augustus
Diogenes Laertius	Life of Archytas
Greek Lyric Poets	Alcaeus, Alcman, Anacreon, Bacchylides, Sappho, Simonides and Stesichorus
Horace	Complete works
Iamblichus	Life of Pythagoras
Ovid	Tristia
Pindar:	Odes
Plato	Laws; Republic
Plutarch	Lives
Porphyrius	Life of Pythagoras
Suetonius	Life of Divine Augustus; Life of Horace
Tacitus	Annals

Guido d'Arezzo
Benedict	Rule of St Benedict
Boethius	Fundamentals of Music
Guido d'Arezzo	Prologue to the Antiphoner; Regulae Rhythmicae; Aliae Regulae; Micrologus; Epistola de ignoto cantu
Paul the Deacon	Versus in laudem Sancti Iohannis Baptistae

Secondary Sources

Horace

Armstrong, D.	Horace	Yale	1989
Bonavia-Hunt, N	Horace the Minstrel	Roundwood	1969
Cambridge			
Ancient History Volume X		Cambridge	1952
Carnabuci, E.	Auditorium di Mecenate	Rome	2005
Gorman, P.	Pythagoras – A Life	Routledge	1979
Graves, R.	The Greek Myths	Penguin	1962
Horatian Society Addresses			1995–2005
Jowett, B.	Dictionary of Greek and		
	Roman Antiquities (Musica)	Murray	1873
Landels, J.G.	Music in Ancient Greece		
	& Rome	Routledge	1999
Last, H.	Social Policy of Augustus (CAH)	Cambridge	1952
Lempriere, J.	Bibliotheca Classica	London	1801
Lonsdale, J.; Lee, S.	Works of Horace	Macmillan	1900
Lyons, S.R.	The Fleeting Years	Staffordshire	1996
Murray, O.	Symposium and Genre in the		
	Poetry of Horace	Duckworth	1993
Nisard. T.	Musique des Odes d'Horace	Zurich	1852
Nisbet, R.G.M.	Romanae Fidicen Lyrae	Routledge	1962
Quinn, K.	Horace – The Odes	Nelson	1980
Shatzman, I.	Senatorial Wealth and		
	Roman Politics	Brussels	1975
Smith, W.	Dictionary of Greek and		
	Roman Antiquities (2nd ed.)	Murray	1873
Syme, R.	The Augustan Aristocracy	Clarendon	1989
	The Roman Revolution	Oxford	1962
Wallace-Hadrill, A.	Suetonius	Duckworth	1983
West, D.	Horace Odes I – Carpe Diem	Clarendon	1995
West, M.L.	Ancient Greek Music	Clarendon	1994
Wilkinson, L.P.	Horace and his Lyric Poetry	Cambridge	1968

Guido d'Arezzo

Abraham, G.	Concise Oxford History of Music	Oxford	1985
Adler, G.	Handbuch des Musichgeschichte	Berlin	1930
Angeloni, L.	Sopra Guido d'Arezzo:		
	dissertazione	Paris	1811
Billanovich, G.	Pomposa Monasterium modo in		
	Italia primum	Padua	1994
Caselli, L.	L'Abbazia di Pomposa	Canova	1996
Dictionnaire de Biographie Francaise		Paris	1959
Duffy, E.	Saints and Sinners	Yale	1997
Fichtenau, H.	Living in the Tenth Century	Chicago	1991
Gillingham, B.	Secular Medieval Latin Song		
	(3 volumes)	Ottawa	1993–98
Kirk, G.S.			
and Raven, J.E.	The Presocratic Philosophers	Cambridge	1962
Palisca, C.V.	Hucbald, Guido & John on Music	Yale	1978
Reston, J.R.	The Last Apocalypse	Doubleday	1998
Samaratini, A.	Presenza Monastica ed Ecclesiale		
	di Pomposa nell'Italia		
	settentrionale sec X–XIV	Corbo	1996
Southern, R.W.	The Making of the Middle Ages	Pimlico	1993
Strunk, O.	Source Readings in Music History	New York	1998
Teitler, L.	Editor of Strunk (*q.v.*)		
Thompson, J.W.	The Medieval Library	New York	1965
Vauchez, A.	The Birth of Christian Europe (from		
	Cambridge Illustrated History of		
	The Middle Ages 950–1250)	Cambridge	1997
Yudkin, J.	Music in Medieval Europe	Prentice-Hall	1989
Zarlino, G.	On the Modes	Yale	1983

Note on Research

I have kept this book free of footnotes to broaden its appeal. I must, however, acknowledge the work of others, while indicating where my research and conclusions are original.

In Chapter 1 *Horace and the Augustan Age*, the descriptions of Horace and his life, education and background are taken from Suetonius's Life of Horace and from his own writings. The quotations from the letters to Horace from Augustus are from Suetonius. For the history of Augustus and his age, including the brief biographies in the Glossary of Proper Names, I have relied mainly on Syme's *The Roman Revolution* and *The Augustan Aristocracy*, the *Cambridge Ancient History* (vol X), and their sources. The events at Cape Palinurus are reported by Dio Cassius in his *Roman History* (49.1.3). I believe I may be the only scholar to have drawn the triple connection between the Palinurus of Horace, Virgil and Dio Cassius.

The story of Murena depends as much on interpretation as on reported history. I am sceptical of the received story. It is not certain that Murena was involved in a plot with Fannius Caepio. The reasons for Augustus wanting to get rid of him are obvious. Horatian scholars have tended to understate the impact of this crisis on the publication and reception of the first three books of odes.

In Chapter 2 *Horace the Songwriter*, I am not the only person to have argued that Horace was a musician, but until the last ten years this has been a rare and unfashionable case to put. The need to redress the balance became apparent to me in 1996 shortly after my book *The Fleeting Years* had gone to the publishers. Reviewing the published material on Horace, I found that despite the internal and external evidence book after book, paper after paper, either ignored or denied the possibility of Horace the songwriter. I must acknowledge *Horace the Minstrel* by the late Noel Bonavia-Hunt, whose brief first chapter presented the case, albeit haphazardly. The dust-cover challenged his musical argument: "Not many Horatian experts would go along with this view: indeed nearly all refute it categorically."

Evidence of Benjamin Jowett's understanding of ancient music is in his long article on *Musica* in *A Dictionary of Greek and Roman Antiquities* (London, 1842). Enoch Powell's remarks are recorded in the *Horatian Society Addresses*. The references to Greek authors are Plato *Laws* 812d and *Republic* 3.10, Aristophanes *Knights* 985 ff and Aristotle *Politics* 1339 ff.

In July 1998, I delivered an address to the Horatian Society in London, setting out my preliminary arguments for Horace as a songwriter. Since then, I have detected a gradual, but incomplete, shift in academic opinion. The significance of the Auditorium of Maecenas came to my attention through the 1985 paper of Oswyn Murray, reprinted as part of the Horace 2000 series under the title *Symposium and Genre in the Poetry of Horace*. The perception that the apse contained a water feature came from a personal visit and information in Elisabetta Carnabuci's leaflet *Auditorium di Mecenate* published by the Comune di Roma.

In my research, while drawing on publicly available material, I have tried to make a fresh contribution to the understanding of Horace. I have pulled together the internal evidence for music in the *carmina* themselves, although I have omitted some examples so as not to overload and irritate the reader. There are some 40 references to music and musical instruments in the Odes. I have drawn fresh attention to the *Carmen Saeculare* as a powerful element in the case for Horace's music, and collected supporting evidence concerning its performance. My discoveries about Archytas are not new, but my conjecture that Horace was interested in him as a musical scientist is. There is a *Life of Archytas* by Diogenes Laertes and several modern commentaries including an article in *Encyclopaedia Britannica*. I have argued the continuity of sung lyric poetry from pre-Classical Greece to Europe at the end of the Dark Ages. More research is needed on this, but there is compelling evidence in Abraham and Gillingham.

The position of Augustus and Agrippa as heads of the *quindecimviri* is recorded in the inscription CIL VI.32323 and noted by Syme in *The Augustan Aristocracy* (p 47). The *Fontes Iuris Anteiustiniani* (I.40) provide a full calendar of the Secular Games of 17 BC, setting out both the sacrificial duties of Augustus and Agrippa, and authenticating Horace as the composer of the *Carmen Saeculare* which was sung by a choir in two locations.

My work on Chapter 3 *Guido d'Arezzo and the Do-re-mi Mystery* began when I started browsing through reference literature on music to see if I could shed further light on Horace's music. Gerald Abraham in the *Oxford Concise History of Music* wrote: "Guido borrowed the setting, in Montpellier M425, of the Horatian ode (IV.11) ... changed the first seven notes ... and fitted the music to a well-known hymn to St. John."[1] It took several months of further investigation before I could conclude that the attribution was right, but the supposed alteration was not. It is a mark of the failure of

---

[1] 1985 edition, p 84.

communication between classicists, musicologists and musical historians that Abraham's remark did not lead to further analysis and challenge. One does not borrow a piece of music for a purpose as specific as Guido's if it is then necessary to change it. It is either fit for purpose or one looks elsewhere.

Theodor Nisard, a research student, wrote a brief essay on the M425 music which was printed at the back of a French language edition of Horace in the mid-nineteenth century.[2] He refers to the *Essai sur la musique ancienne et moderne* (Vol II, p 43) by Laborde, which asserted that the Romans sang almost all their poetry and noted that the Horatian ode had been "adapted" for the Hymn. Nisard noted the lack of evidence for Laborde's assertions and transposition, but correctly recognised the connection between the Ode to Phyllis and Guido's setting of *ut queant laxis*. However, his own musical interpretation was also faulty. His essay was not widely read and for the next eighty years little academic interest was shown in M425.

In 1930 Guido Adler noted the survival of six musical fragments for Horatian odes.[3] He added that the melody of IV.11 at Montpellier was "die gleiche Melodie wie die als Schulmelodie der Solmisation benutzte Melodie des Hymnus *Ut queant laxis* aufweis." He made no reference to Guido d'Arezzo, however. M425 was listed, with an accompanying illustration, in the *Catalogue General des Manuscrits des Bibliotheques Publiques*[4] and described as 10th century quarto on vellum.

For several decades, Groves Music Dictionary, used as a reputable source of information by many students and lovers of music, promoted many errors concerning Guido's innovation and life history, and declared: "It is probable that Guido invented the melody as a mnemonic device or reworked an existing melody now lost."[5]

Bryan Gillingham of the Institute of Medieval Music in Ottawa[6] published a transposition of the music of the M425 Ode to Phyllis onto a treble stave, but was not aware, until I spoke to him, of any connection with Guido d'Arezzo.

---

[2] Orellius edition (Zurich 1852) vol II, pp 922–935.
[3] Handbuch der Musikgeschichte (Berlin 1930) vol I, p 160. Apart from IV.11, the odes are I.1, I.3, I.33, III.9 and III.13. I.1 is a poor gloss in Vat Reg Lat 1703, f 3. I.3 appears as an 11th century gloss in Vat Reg Lat 1672, f 2, and in Reg Lat 1703, f 4. I.33 is a marginal addition, written sideways in M 425. I have not been able to trace III.9 or III.13.
[4] Paris 1849, vol I.
[5] Article by Claude V. Palisca, date unknown.
[6] Secular Medieval Latin Song (Ottawa 1993), vol I.

Gillingham's work was careful and of considerable value, but had one serious difficulty. He transposed the musical line of the diastematic neumes accurately, but chose a pitch for the Ode to Phyllis that was one third higher than that of the Hymn to St John. This made it impossible for researchers relying on his work to observe the perfect match between the two tunes and led to the same sort of conclusion reached by Gerald Abraham. This caused a temporary setback in my research, until I developed a better understanding of this system of musical notation.

I was able, with the help of Richard Andrewes, head of music at the Cambridge University Library, to arrive at an accurate reading of the M425 neumes. In 1998, Andrewes confirmed that the melody for the second stanza of Horace ("multa qua crines") was identical with Guido's "ut queant laxis". Early in 2006, he confirmed that the other stanzas followed the same pattern, with minor musical variations or embellishments. I then worked through the neumes note by note proving to my satisfaction that the melody was precisely what Guido had used for his ut-re-mi mnemonic and that he had had no need to adjust it. I have dated M425 by reference to the style of its Carolingian minuscule script, confirming the assessment of the *Catalogue General* that it is tenth century. In my view it was written in the middle of the century rather than at the end and certainly preceded Guido's birth. I have established from the MS that the music was not a later interpolation but contemporaneous with the text, and explained why, if this particular manuscript was his source, Guido used the music from the second stanza. I have confirmed that both the Ode and the Hymn were written in Horatian Sapphics, a conclusion that could not be drawn from Abraham due to an error in his text.[7] I have found no record of the Horatian music being used in any previous version of the Hymn to St John, and Guido used it only in the first stanza.

My study of Guido took me to Pomposa, Arezzo and Rome. By reading Guido's own writings, the Italian studies listed in the Bibliography and broader accounts of medieval history, I have been able to reconstruct some of his travels and conversations, and deduce from his character, tribulations and the religious climate of the day why he used the words of a Benedictine hymn as an "envelope" for the music of a Horatian ode. This is at the heart of the Mystery of Do-re-mi. I hope the story will provide fresh insight for musicologists and musical and medieval historians.

James Reston Jr in *The Last Apocalypse* (chapters 10 and 12) describes the chaotic and dangerous political and religious environment in Italy

---

[7] op.cit. p 82: "labi" for "labii".

around 1000 AD, with particular reference to Otto III and his controversial pope Sylvester II, originally Gerbert d'Aurillac the former archbishop of Ravenna. For the renewal of independence for the Monastery of Pomposa and its emergence under Abbot Guido degli Strambiati, I have relied mainly on Samaritani's excellent *Presenza Monastica ed Ecclesiale di Pomposa*. I have, however, resisted depending on his scholarly speculations concerning dates and movements in Guido d'Arezzo's life. It is sufficient for the purposes of my story to use Guido's own writings. The description of the visit to Pope John XIX is as Guido describes it. The information about John's background and the visit of King Canute comes from Eamon Duffy's *Saints and Sinners* (p 86).

My source for corruption at the Cathedral church at Arezzo is Southern's *The Making of the Middle Ages* (pp 124–7). For decades its custodians were a single extended family who profiteered from extortionate sales to pilgrims of bread and candles that had been purchased and donated by others.

Details of Paul the Deacon's life come from the *Catholic Encyclopaedia*. The full text of his Latin poems is taken from the Bibliotheca Augustana in Augsburg.

The life of Jean-Antoine Chaptal is featured in the *Dictionnaire de Biographie Francaise* (1959 edition, vol VIII) and further details of the journey of M425, including the role of Prunelle and the history of Pithou, were furnished in a brochure of the Medical Library at Monpellier.

Finally, all the verse translations in this volume, including those of Virgil and Paul the Deacon, are mine.

Glossary of Proper Names

Academy: Socratic school in Athens

Achaean car: two-wheeled racing chariot designed on traditional Greek lines.

Achaemenes: ancestor of kings of Persia.

Acherontia: settlement on Mount Voltur.

Achilles: son of Thetis; Greek warrior hero of Trojan War, subject of Homer's *Iliad*; dressed in girl's clothes at Scyros to escape detection.

Acrisius: father of Danae; told by Oracle that he would have no sons, but his grandson would kill him; imprisoned Danae, but killed by discus wound caused by grandson Perseus.

Actium: sea battle 31 BC when Octavian defeated Antony and Cleopatra.

Aeacus: judge of shades of the dead.

Aeneas: Trojan hero celebrated in Virgil's *Aeneid*; son of Venus and Anchises; father of Ascanius; mythical founder of Rome.

Aeolia: part of coastal Asia Minor opposite island of Lesbos; Aeolian is used of songs of Alcaeus and Sappho, written and sung in Aeolian dialect.

Aeolus: god of winds; charged by Jupiter to keep winds imprisoned in caverns until instructed to release them.

Agamemnon: son of Atreus, king of Mycenae, brother of Menelaus; leader of Greek forces at Troy; sacrificed daughter Iphigenia; lover of prophetess Cassandra; murdered by wife Clytemnestra and her lover Aegisthus.

Agrippa: (63–12 BC) Marcus Vipsanius Agrippa, commander of Octavian's forces, builder of Augustan Rome; praetor 40 BC, consul 37 BC; military success over Sextus Pompeius in 36 BC brought him estates in Sicily managed by Iccius; aedile 33 BC repairing public buildings and distributing oil and wine; properties in Egypt and on Palatine Hill following defeat of Antony; owned area of Campus Martius, creating gardens and baths; constructed buildings throughout Italy and Gaul, including Pantheon and Saepta Julia in Rome; owned Thracian Chersonnese; joint consul with Augustus 28 and 27 BC; joint leader of Fifteen Men (college of priests); further joint powers with Augustus after 23; married Augustus' daughter Julia 21 BC after death of Marcellus; joint celebrant with Augustus of Ludi Saeculares 17 BC; died 12 BC.

Ajax: son of Telemon; Greek hero in Trojan War, noted for great bravery.

Alban Hills: hills south of Rome; also site of Alban Lake; Mount Albanus is today's Monte Cavo.

Albunea: spring near Tibur gushing up between high rocks to form waterfall.

Alcaeus: lyric poet of Lesbos, flourished 610 BC; model for Horace's Alcaeic metre; supported radical movement in civil war against tyrants.

Alexandria: Egyptian capital of Cleopatra where she and Antony died; surrendered to Rome in August 30 BC.

Algidus: wooded mountain in Alban Hills; today's Monte Compatri.

Alyattes: rich king of Lydia in Asia Minor; father of Croesus.

Amphiaraus: Argive prophet (III.16); husband of Eriphyle, who was bribed by promise of magic necklace to persuade him to join Seven Against Thebes expedition led by her brother Adrastus king of Argos.

Amphion: son of Antiope who was seduced by Jupiter and produced twins, the other being Zethus; as adults they visited Thebes, their mother's birthplace and ejected king, rebuilding walls of lower city; Amphion received a lyre from Mercury: the stones moved to the sound and slid into place.

Anacreon: Greek lyric poet, born Teos, fl 570 BC.

Anchises: father of Aeneas, who rescued him from Troy by carrying him on back.

Ancus: fourth of legendary kings of ancient Rome.

Andromeda: daughter of king Cephaleus of Ethiopia, who had her bound to a rock; rescued from sea-monster by Perseus, who married her; all three finally placed among stars.

Anio: river near Tibur outside Rome.

Antilochus: son of Nestor; killed by Memnon in Trojan War.

Antiochus: Syrian king defeated by Roman general Scipio Africanus in 190 BC.

Antony: Marcus Antonius; supporter of Julius Caesar; consul 44 BC; proconsul of Cisalpine Gaul; triumvir with Octavian and Lepidus; married (1) Fulvia, (2) Octavia; victor at Philippi; Peace of Brundisium with Octavian; lover of Cleopatra; defeated at Actium; suicide 30 BC; see Chapter 1.

Apollo: sun god, son of Jupiter and Lato; temple of Apollo dedicated on Palatine Hill 9 October 28 BC.

Apennines: mountain range down spine of Italy, inhabited by Paeligni, descendants of Sabines.

April: month connected with Venus of the Sea, possibly derived from Greek *aphros* (= foam).

Aquilo: north wind.

Arcadia: mountainous region of northern Peloponnese, noted for idyllic beauty.

Archytas: (c 400–350 BC) b Tarentum; subject of I.28; mathematician and acoustic scientist, contemporary of Plato; taught at school of Pythagoras in Croton, southern Italy; murdered on Matine coast; for significance, see Chapter 2.

Arcturus: brightest star in constellation Bootes, whose evening setting in October portended stormy weather.

Argive: the Argive prophet (III.16) is Amphiaraus, *qv*.

Ariadne: daughter of Minos of Crete; saved Theseus from labyrinth; abandoned by him at Naxos where Bacchus fell in love with her.

Aristius: see Fuscus.

Armenia: country ceded to Octavian after battle of Actium, becoming vassal state of Rome.

Asia Minor: territory covered by today's western Turkey.

Asinius: Asinius Pollio, *qv*.

Assyria: area of Middle East that included vale of Jericho, where nard was grown for hairdressing and body lotion.

Asterie: girl's name (III.7) sometimes connected with island of Rhodes.

Atlas: god who supported heavens from mountains of north-west Africa; "Atlas' bounds" (I.34) may refer to limits of known world.

Atreus: see Thyestes.

Atrides: son of Atreus; surname of Agamemnon.

Attalus: Attalus III of Pergamos, famed for wealth, said to have invented weaving of gold fabric.

Attica: country of which Athens was capital; Attic (or Cecropian) shoe was buskin worn by tragic actors.

Aufidus: river about ten miles from Venusia.

Aufula: settlement between Tibur and Praeneste

Augustus: b 63 BC, Augustus Caesar, otherwise Octavius or Octavian; adopted son of Julius Caesar; married (1) Scribonia, by whom he had a daughter Julia; married (2) Livia, *qv.*; brother of Octavia; for career and relationship with Horace, see Chapter 1.

Aulon: mountain near Tarentum.

Ausonian Sea: sea between Iapygian peninsula and Straits of Sicily.

Auster: south wind.

Aventine: one of Rome's seven hills, site of ancient temple to Diana.

Babylon: Parthian centre of ancient mathematics and astrology.

Bacchantes: female revellers, worshippers of Bacchus.

Bacchus: god of wine, ecstasy and the irrational, son of Semele by Jupiter; also known as Dionysus or Bassareus.

Baiae: fashionable coastal resort on northern Bay of Naples, around which were senatorial estates, including one inherited by Augustus from Julius Caesar.

Bandusia: spring near Horace's farm, where libations of wine and offerings of flowers marked festival of *Fontinalia* at end July at rising of constellation Canicula or Lesser Dog.

Bantia: settlement on Mount Voltur.

Barine: name of freedwoman in II.8 (three syllables).

Basque: anachronistic translation of the Concanus tribe of northern Spain.

Bassareus: alternative name for Bacchus.

Bassus: see Damalis. In Nero's reign, Caesius Bassus was a lyric poet, but there is no evidence he was related to Horace's friend.

Bellerophon: rider of winged horse Pegasus, sent by Proteus to Iobates who was instructed to kill him; succeeded at potentially fatal missions; after slaying Chimaera, tried to fly to heaven but was thrown off by Pegasus; Iobates discovering his innocence, gave him his daughter Philonoe; see Proteus.

Berecyntus: mountain in Asia Minor sacred to Cybele, to whom name Berecyntia is given; Berecyntian pipe is curved flute from Phrygia.

Bibulus: Marcus Calpurnius Bibulus, Roman consul 59 BC; pun (bibulous) is intended in Latin as in English.

Bistonids: Thracian Bacchantes.

Bithynia: province of Asia Minor between Bosporus and Black Sea.

Breuni: people of Rhaetia, Germany, adjacent to Genauni.

Briseis: slave girl taken from Achilles by Agamemnon, causing Achilles to withdraw from fighting until death of his friend Patroclus.

Brutus: Marcus Junius Brutus; praetor 44 BC; assassin of Julius Caesar; recruited Horace as junior officer in Athens; suicide after second Battle of Philippi 42 BC; for further details, see Chapter 1.

Caecubum: area in southern Latium noted for fine wine.

Calabria: region of southern Italy; "Muses of Calabria" (IV.8) refers to Roman poet Ennius, author of Annals, which celebrated victory in Second Punic War.

Calais: son of Ornytus from Thurii; Calais is pronounced with three syllables.

Cales: town in southern Campania noted for wine, today's Calvi; adjective Calenian.

Calliope: Chief of Muses; goddess of poetry.

Camena: Roman or Latin Muse.

Camillus: Marcus Furius Camillus, dictator 396 BC; second founder of Rome after its recovery from Gauls.

Campania: fertile Italian province around Naples.

Campus: Campus Martius (Field of Mars), Roman park and sports ground where Rome's officials were elected.

Cantabrians: people of north-west Spain; resisted Augustus 26 BC; subdued by Agrippa 19 BC.

Capitol: Capitoline Hill in Rome or Temple of Jupiter Capitolinus on hill.

Caria: region of Asia Minor, south of Lydia.

Carpathian Sea: sea in southern Aegean between Crete and Rhodes.

Carthaginians: usually identified with Carthage, but originated in Phoenicia in eastern Mediterranean and settled in Spain as well as north Africa.

Caspian: sea in Asia.

Castalia: spring on Mount Parnassus in Greece sacred to Apollo and the Muses.

Castor: Castor and Pollux, twin sons of Leda by Jupiter; stars and divine protectors of seafarers; temple in Rome first dedicated in 484 BC.

Catilus: son of Amphiaraus; builder of walls of Tibur.

Cato: Marcus Porcius Cato ("the younger"); senator famed for fortitude and high-minded stoicism; supporter of Pompey, committed suicide after Julius Caesar's victory at Thapsus in 46 BC.

Cato: Marcus Porcius Cato the Censor: consul 195 BC; censor of Rome; farmer, statesman and moralist.

Caucasus: mountains between Black Sea and Caspian Sea.

Cea: Latin name for Ceos; island off Cape Sunium at tip of Attica, one of Cyclades; birthplace of Greek lyric poet Simonides.

Cecrops: ancient king, founder of acropolis of Athens.

Censorinus: Caius Marcius Censorinus; addressee of IV.8; consul 8 BC, died as proconsul in east.

Centaur: mythical creature with man's head and lion's body; foe of Lapiths.

Ceos: Greek name of Cea, *qv.*

Cerberus: hundred-headed dog who guarded entrance to underworld but was subdued by sound of Orpheus' lyre.

Ceres: goddess of agriculture, particularly cereal crops.

Charon: ferryman of dead across River Styx.

Chimaera: fire-breathing monster, part lion, part dragon and part goat.

Chios: Aegean island off coast of Ionia in Asia Minor.

Chloe: girl's name (I.23).

Chloris: girl's name (III.15), wife of Ibycus.

Cinara: lover of Horace; died prematurely.

Circe: sea nymph with magical powers; lover of Odysseus.

Claudius: Caius Claudius Nero; led forced march 207 BC to River Metaurus to defeat Hasdrubal, brother of Hannibal, turning course of Second Punic War.

Claudius: see Tiberius.

Cleopatra: Queen of Egypt, mistress of Julius Caesar; mistress later of Antony who bequeathed to her and her sons Rome's eastern territories, precipitating war with Senate; defeated by Octavian at Actium 31 BC; suicide in Alexandria 10 September 30 BC; see Odes I.37 *"nunc est bibendum"* and Chapter 1.

Clio: Greek Muse of history.

Cnidos: Carian centre of worship for Venus, with statue by fifth-century Athenian sculptor Praxiteles.

Codrus: last king of Athens, gave himself voluntarily to death to give his people victory over Spartans.

Colchis: east of Black Sea, site of Golden Fleece and birthplace of Medea, wife of Jason the Argonaut and killer of their children; site of two fire-breathing bulls harnessed by Jason to sew serpents' teeth, which turned into armed men.

Concanus: see Basque.

Consul: highest civil officer in Roman republic; two consuls served together for one year, having moved through various junior magistracies on *cursus honorum* and reached age 43.

Corinth: city on Greek isthmus.

Corvinus: Marcus Valerius Messalla Corvinus; high-spending student in Athens with Horace 45 BC; joined Brutus's forces; part source for Plutarch's Life of Brutus; naval command under Octavian in Sicilian War; successful campaigns against Dalmatians in Illyria 34 BC; commanded part fleet at Actium; consul 31 BC replacing Antony; campaigned Gaul 27 BC, awarded triumph; used booty to reconstruct Via Latina and decorate Rome; awarded part of Antony's estate on Palatine Hill; member of Fifteen Men; responsible for Rome's aqueducts 11 BC; noted orator and wine-drinker; sponsor of Tibullus.

Corybantes: priests of Cybele whose worship included wild music and dance.

Cos: Sporadic island in Sea of Myrtos off coast of Caria.

Cotiso: king of Dacians near River Danube; perhaps "king of the northern shore" (I.26).

Cragos: mountain chain in Lycia.

Crassus: member of First Triumvirate with Pompey the Great and Julius Caesar; known for wealth, invaded Parthia 53 BC with 35,000 men, defeated by 10,000 Parthian archers, and killed ingloriously.

Crete: Mediterranean island, with chalk was noted for whiteness; to mark in Cretan chalk (I.36) is like modern "red letter day."

Crispus: Sallustius Crispus; addressee of II.2; adopted son and great-nephew of historian Sallust; succeeded Maecenas as Augustus' chief domestic and political adviser 23 BC; probably nephew of C. Sallustius Crispus, praetor 46 BC, known for high living and heavy debts when young, and for bribes, embezzlement and confiscations when proconsul in Africa 46–45 BC; see Chapter 1.

Cumae: ancient colony of Chalcidians established in Campania.

Curius: Marcus Curius Dentatus, consul 290 and 275 BC; defeated Pyrrhus at Battle of Beneventum.

Cybele: see Vesta.

Cyclades: group of islands in Aegean Sea.

Cyclopes: one-eyed giants working in Vulcan's smithy.

Cynthius: name for Apollo.

Cyprus: Mediterranean island, known for Temple of Venus.

Cyrus: king of Asia Minor; also young man's name.

Cytherean: description of Venus, after Cythera, Aegean island noted for her worship.

Dacians: inhabitants of today's Romania.

Daedalus: father of Icarus.

Dalmatians: people inhabiting eastern coast of Adriatic Sea.

Damalis: female friend of Bassus, competing in *amystis* (I.36), drinking contest in which goblet is drained at single gulp.

Damocles, sword of: suspended over the subject's neck on order of Dionysus, tyrant of Syracuse in Sicily, Damocles being one of his courtiers.

Danaans: alternative name for Greeks of pre-classical period.

Danae: daughter of Acrisius, who imprisoned her for her protection (III.16); Jupiter hid in shower of gold and fathered Perseus, who as adult threw discus at funeral games in Larissa, hitting grandfather's foot and causing death from injury.

Danaus: originally king of Libya, later king in Greece; founder of Danaans; built citadel of Argos; his twin brother Aegyptus of Egypt, had fifty sons, Danaus fifty daughters; to settle feud it was agreed cousins would marry, but Danaus told daughters to kill husbands on wedding night with pins hidden in hair; Hypermnestra spared her husband, the other sisters were condemned to carry water in underworld in leaky jars (III.13).

Dardanus: son of Zeus and Electra; ancestor of Priam and Trojans.

Daunia: Roman province in central Italy named after King Daunus.

Death's goddess: Libitina; goddess of dead bodies; all products required for burial and funerals were sold in her temple, and the register of deaths kept there.

Deiphobus: son of Priam and Hecuba of Troy.

Dellius: Quintus Dellius; addressee of II.3; described as *desultor* in civil wars – circus performer vaulting between horses; diplomatic missions for Antony in Syria; transferred allegiance to Octavian before Actium; wrote history of Antony's Parthian campaign.

Delos: Aegean island sacred to Apollo; Delian foliage refers to garlands of laurel sacred to Apollo.

Delphi: home of Oracle and Pythian Games, above northern shore of Gulf of Corinth, sacred to Apollo; Delphic laurel is laurel or bay of Apollo.

Diana: daughter of Jupiter and Lato; goddess of hunting, Greek Artemis; holy day Ides (13th) of August; sometimes represented in triple form with three heads, for earthly role as huntress, heavenly role as moon goddess, and underworld role as Hecate; also goddess of birth and chastity.

Dindymene: Vesta or Cybele; epithet refers to shrine on Mt Dindymon in northern Asia Minor.

Diomedes: son of Tydeus; Greek warrior hero of Trojan War.

Dirce: fountain of Thebes in Boeotia; swan of Dirce is name for Pindar.

Drusus: (38–9 BC); praised in IV.4 and IV.14; son of Livia, stepson of Augustus, brother of Tiberius; born three months after mother's marriage to Octavian, possibly fathered by her first husband Tiberius Claudius Nero.

Earth, children of: Titans, Giants who rebelled against Jupiter.

Enipeus: lover of Asterie; name recalls rivers in Thessaly and Pieria.

Ephesus: commercial city on coast of Ionia with temple to Diana.

Ephialtes: see Otus.

Epirus: part of today's Albania.

Erymanthus: range of mountains in Arcadia in northern Peloponnese.

Eryx: home in Sicily of famous temple to Venus.

Esquiline Hill: one of Rome's seven hills, location of Maecenas's palace and auditorium, and later of his and Horace's graves.

Ethiopians: troops used by Cleopatra against Rome.

Euhius: name for Bacchus, probably derived from cry of joy.

Eumenides: euphemistic name for Furies (= kindly ones).

Euphorbus: warrior in Trojan War, from whom Pythagoras claimed reincarnation.

Europa: born near Tyre, daughter of Agenor; Jupiter fell in love with her and disguised himself as gentle snow-white bull; after she climbed on his back, he swam to Crete and ravished her; mother of Minos, judge of underworld.

Euterpe: Greek Muse of dance.

Eurus: south east wind.

Fabricius: consul 281 and 278 BC; led Romans against Pyrrhus 280 BC.

Falernian: vintage from area of Campania.

Faunus: protecting deity of agriculture and shepherds, identified with Greek god Pan with horns and goats' feet; "special December day" was the Nones, falling on fifth of month (III.18).

Fifteen Men: *quindecimviri*, college of priests in charge of Sybilline Books, from which they divined religious means of averting danger to city of Rome.

Forentum: settlement on Mount Voltur.

Formiae: wine-growing area in hills near coast of Latium; location of Murena family estate.

Fuscus: Aristius Fuscus; addressee of I.22; amusing friend of Horace, also appearing in *Epistles* and *Satires* .

Gaetulia: region identified with today's Morocco.

Galaesus: river near Tarentum, where fleeces were considered so valuable that sheep were protected with leather skins.

Galatea: friend of Horace about to return to Greece (III.27); names recalls myth of sea nymph Galatea who loved Acis, river god, son of Faunus, but Polyphemus the Cyclops was in love with her and killed Acis in fit of jealousy.

Gelonians: tribe of Scythia in today's Ukraine.

Genaunians: Germanic people in Raetia; see Raeti.

Getae: Thracian tribe living near River Danube.

Geryon: mythical giant with three bodies living in far west.

Glycera: female name from Greek for "sweet".

Goat Star: *Capra*, star in constellation Auriga.

Grosphus: Pompeius Grosphus, addressee of II.16, introduced by Horace to Iccius in Epistles I.12; probably lived in Sicily.

Gyas: a giant.

Gyges: boy's name; beautiful adolescent from Cnidos in Caria (II.5); lover of Asterie (III.7); originally name of a king of Lydia, famous for ring that made him invisible.

Hadria: Adriatic Sea.

Haemus: mountain range in Thrace where mythical singer Orpheus lived.

Hannibal: Carthaginian enemy of Rome in Second Punic War 208–201 BC, invading from Alps with elephants before withdrawing.

Hebrus: river in Thrace.

Hector: greatest of Trojan heroes in Trojan War; killed by Achilles.

Helicon: mountain in Boeotia sacred to Apollo and Muses.

Hercules: demigod famous for Labours; called on by Jupiter to kill Giants, it being ordained that no Giant could be killed by a god; slew Geryon in Spain.

Hermes: Greek name for Mercury, *qv.*

Hesperia: Italy, land of the west.

Hippolyte: born in Magnesia, Thessaly; wife of Acastus of Iolcus, attempted seduction of Peleus whom Acastus then tried to have killed by Centaurs; see Peleus.

Hippolytus: son of Theseus; his stepmother Phaedra fell in love with him and, unrequited, made accusations to her husband who cursed him; torn to pieces by his horses.

Hirpinus: Quinctius Hirpinus; addressee of II.11; member of well-known provincial family in Samnium.

Hister: lower part of River Danube.

Holy Shields: dating from time of Numa Pompilius, second king of Rome; kept in Temple of Mars.

Hyades: group of seven stars in constellation Taurus.

Hydaspes: tributary of River Indus.

Hydra: mythical water monster killed by Hercules; originally had seven heads, but when one was cut off, another two grew in its place.

Hylaeus: Centaur who tried to rape Atalanta but was shot by her.

Hymettus: mountain near Athens, famed for honeybees and marble.

Iapyx: westerly and north-westerly wind blowing from Italy to Greece.

Iberia: Spain.

Icarus: son of Daedalus; flying from Crete with father, went too close to sun, causing wax on wings to melt, leading to death in Icarian sea.

Iccius: friend of Horace, addressee of I.31; probably planned to join Arabian campaign of Aelius Gallus 26 BC; reappears in Epistles I.12 as steward in Sicily where he collected rents from Agrippa's estates.

Ida: mountain from which wood was felled for Paris's ships; adjective Idean.

Ides: mid-point in Roman month; Ides of March fell on fifteenth, when Julius Caesar was killed 44 BC; Ides of April on thirteenth, birthday of Maecenas (IV.11).

Idomeneus: king of Crete, led Cretan contingent against Troy.

Ilia: poetic name for Rhea Silvia, mother by Mars of Romulus founder of Rome.

Ilium: name for Troy.

Inachus: first king of Argos in Greece.

Ionia: region of Asia Minor noted for supposed moral laxity.

Isthmian Games: games celebrated at Corinth.

Itys: son of Tereus and Procne, killed by mother and boiled in cauldron for father to eat as punishment for adultery; see Tereus and Procne.

Iullus: Iullus Antonius; addressee of IV.2; son of Antony and first wife Fulvia; brought up by Augustus's sister Octavia (Antony's second wife); consul 10 BC.

Ixion: son of Phlegyas, Lapith king; murdered Eioneus, prospective father-in-law, but Jupiter agreed to purify him and invited him to dinner, where Ixion planned to rape Juno; Jupiter, creating false Juno from cloud, suprised Ixion and had him bound to wheel of fire rolling ceaselessly through sky.

Janus: temple at Rome whose doors were closed during peace time

Jove: alternative name for Jupiter.

Jugurtha: usurper of Numidian throne 118 BC; his erratic behaviour led to war with Rome; captured and brought to Rome 105 BC where he met his death.

Juno: sister, wife and principal consort of Jupiter.

Jupiter: king of Olympian gods.

Kalends: *Kalendae* (Latin first line of III.8) is first day of month; 1st March was date of *Matrimonalia* in honour of Juno; Horace, a bachelor, celebrated it as anniversary of survival from falling tree.

Laertes: father of Odysseus.

Laestrygonia: town mentioned in Homer's *Odyssey*, identified with Formiae.

Lalage: real or imaginary love of Horace.

Lamia: Lucius Aelius Lamia; probable addressee of I.26, I.36 and III.17; b 65 BC to senatorial family with interests in property and Africa; Augustus's senior praetorian legate in Spain 24 to 22 BC, responsible for three or four legions near Tarragona. "Lamus" appears in Book 10 of Homer's *Odyssey*.

Lanuvium: town outside Rome en route from Rome to Brundisium; site of one of Augustus's summer homes.

Laomedon: king of Troy and father of Priam; cheated Neptune and Apollo out of their fee for building walls and tending flocks; defrauded Hercules by substituting mortal horses for immortal mares promised for rescuing his daughter Hesione.

Lapiths: mountain tribe, mythical foes of Centaurs.

Lar: household god, plural Lares; tutelary deities of the home (III.23, first stanza; gods in the last stanza are Penates.)

Larissa: town in Thessaly.

Lato or Latona: mother by Jupiter of Apollo and Diana.

Latium: region of central Italy, home of Latin language.

Leda: mother by Jupiter of Castor and Pollux.

Leo: constellation of Lion.

Lesbos: Aegean island of Asia Minor, home of Sappho and Alcaeus, *qv*.

Leuconoe: female name, probably contrived from Greek for "empty-headed."

Liber: ancient Italian deity identified with Bacchus.

Libitina: see Death's goddess.

Licinius: addressee of II.10, possibly Lucius Licinius Varro Murena; see Murena.

Ligurinus: boy's name.

Liris: river between Latium and Campania, today's Garigliano.

Livia: Livia Drusilla; married (1) Tiberius Claudius Nero, (2) Augustus; mother of Tiberius and Drusus.

Lollius: Marcus Lollius; addressee of IV.9; *novus homo* ("new man"); consul 21 BC; replaced as legate in Gaul by Tiberius 16 BC for poor military record.

Luceria: modern Lucera, famous for high quality wool.

Lucius: see Volcacius.

Lucretilis: "lovely hill" near Horace's Sabine farm (I.17).

Lucrine Lake: beauty spot inland from Baiae.

Lyce: female name contrived from Greek for she-wolf (III.10, IV.13); in Latin *lupa* means both she-wolf and prostitute.

Lycaeus: mountain in Arcadia.

Lycia: country in Asia Minor supporting Troy in Trojan war.

Lycidas: boy's name.

Lycoris: girl's name.

Lycurgus: king of Edonians in Thrace, who prohibited worship of Bacchus, ordering subjects to destroy vines, for which he was driven mad; believing son

Dryas to be a vine, killed and pruned him with axe; taken by Edonians at Bacchus' instigation to Mount Pangaeum and torn apart by wild horses.

Lycus: boy's name.

Licymnia: probably pseudonym for Terentia wife of Maecenas (II.12); see Chapter 1.

Lyde: girl's name, in III.11 obdurate young filly and in III.28 servant and musical companion.

Lydia: girl's name, addressee of I.8, I.13 and I.25; participant in love duet III.9; perhaps associated with country of Asia Minor, home of "Lydian flute" (*tibia* – originally made from bone).

Macedonian: the Macedonian (III.16) is Philip II (father of Alexander the Great) famous for bribes; "captains of frigates" two lines later could be veiled criticism of Menas, naval commander under Sextus Pompeius c 36 BC, as he twice reneged on commitments to Octavian.

Maecenas, Caius Cilnius Maecenas: knight, business tycoon and extravagant sponsor of the arts; born in Aretium (Arezzo) of royal ancestry; diplomatic adviser and negotiator for Augustus, exercising power in Rome in his absence, particularly during campaigns of 32–23 BC; close friend and patron of Horace; husband of Terentia, brother-in-law of Murena and Proculeius; addressee of Odes I.1, II.12, II.17, III.8, III.16, III.29 and subject of IV.11; owner of palace compound on Esquiline Hill; fell from power 23 BC; died 8 BC; see Chapter 1.

Maia: consort of Jupiter and mother of Mercury.

Manlius: see Torquatus.

Marcellus: Roman hero in Second Punic War against Carthaginians.

Marcellus: (43–23 BC) Marcus Claudius Marcellus, nephew and intended heir of Augustus, married Augustus's daughter Julia 25 BC; member of Fifteen Men 25 BC; nominated for consulship 23 BC, but name withdrawn (see Chapter 1); died young.

March, Ides of: see Ides.

Marica: nymph in territory of Minturnae on river Liris; mother of Latins.

Mark Antony: Marcus Antonius, see Antony.

Mars: god of war, father of Romulus.

Marsians: Latin people living near Lake Fucinus, subjected to Rome 90 BC.

Massagetae: Scythian people living to east of Caspian Sea, perhaps as far as today's Mongolia.

Massic: highly regarded wine from today's Monte Massico in southern Campania.

Matine: adjective from Mount Matinus near Apulian coast of Italy.

Melpomene: Muse of lyric song.

Memphis: Egyptian city, 14 miles south of today's Cairo, site of a temple of Venus.

Mercury: Greek Hermes, messenger of gods and inventer of lyre; god of banking and commerce, protector of Horace.

Meriones: Greek warrior hero of Trojan War.

Metaurus: river in north-east Italy.

Metellus: consul 60 BC, when First Triumvirate was launched; see Introduction.

Mimas: giant giving name to mountain range in Ionia opposite island of Chios.

Minerva: identified with Pallas Athene, virgin goddess of Athens, but specifically in Rome protectress of chastity and women's crafts, who helped relocate Trojan exiles to Rome.

Minos: son of Jupiter and Europa, judge of shades of the dead in underworld.

Monaeses: Parthian commander; defeated Roman forces in Syria 36 BC.

Morocco: Moroccan sands, see Syrtes.

Munatius: see Plancus.

Murena: Lucius Licinius Varro Murena; brother of Maecenas's wife Terentia; lent Maecenas and Horace house in Formiae on journey to Brundisium 37 BC (Satires I.5); toasted in III.19 on entry to College of Augurs; possibly addressee of II.10 (as "Licinius"); killed after implication in conspiracy against Augustus in 23 BC; see Chapter 1.

Mygdon: legendary prince of Phrygia in Asia Minor.

Myrtale: freedwoman (I.33), actual or imaginary girl friend of Horace (three syllables).

Myrtos, sea of: southern Aegean Sea.

Mytilene: principal city of Lesbos.

Naiad: fresh water nymph.

Nearchus: boy's name, also identified with Alexander the Great's admiral.

Nectar: drink of gods.

Neobule: girl's name, probably contrived from Greek for "new-fangled idea."

Neptune: god of the sea, to whom seafarers offered commemorative plaques on safe return (I.5); the *Neptunalia* holiday was 23 July.

Nereus: Greek sea god, son of Oceanus and Tethys, father of Nereides (I.15).

Nereides: sea nymphs, daughters of Nereus, loyal to Neptune.

Nestor: king of Pylos, father of Antilochus; Greek seer known for wisdom and prophecies in Trojan War.

Night-Shiner: name for Diana as goddess of the moon.

Niobe: wife of king Amphion of Thebes, with seven sons and seven daughters; punished for boasting superiority over Lato, who had only two children, Apollo and Diana, who killed Niobe's children with arrows; turned into weeping stone, identified with rock near Mount Sipylus in today's Turkey.

Niphates: mountain in Armenia.

Numantia: region of north-west Spain resisting Rome from 195 BC until capture in 133 BC.

Numida: friend of Horace and Lamia; addressee of I.36.

Numidia: region identified with modern Libya.

Octavius, also Octavian and Augustus, *qv*; see also Chapter 1.

Odysseus: son of Laertes, husband of Penelope, father of Telemachus; king of Ithaca; Greek warrior hero of Trojan War, subject of Homer's *Odyssey*; lover of Circe.

Olympus: mountain of gods on border of Macedonia and Thessaly.

Opus: town in Locris in Greece.

Orcus: name for underworld and Pluto its king.

Oricum: Adriatic port south of Brundisium.

Orion: hunter who tried to assault Diana, but was shot by her and transported to heaven as constellation setting in stormy season of November.

Orpheus: mythical minstrel from Thrace; husband of Eurydice.

Otus: son, with brother Ephialtes, of Iphimedeia by Neptune; they grew one fathom in height and one cubit in length every year, declaring war on gods when nine years old; tried to drop Mount Pelion on Mount Olympus; attempting to kill Diana in form of white doe, they shot one another dead with spears.

Pacorus: Parthian commander victorious against Romans in Syria and southern Asia Minor c 40 BC before being killed 38 BC.

Palatine: one of Rome's seven hills.

Palinurus: cape on Tyrrhenian Sea in south-west Italy (III.4) where Horace escaped death, probably accompanying Maecenas with Octavian's fleet in defeat at sea by Sextus Pompeius 38 BC; see Chapter 1.

Pan: see Faunus.

Panaetius: 1st century BC Stoic philosopher.

Paphos: centre of worship for Venus in Cyprus.

Paris: son of King Priam of Troy; stole Helen from Menelaus of Sparta, precipitating Trojan War; earlier, judged beauty contest between goddesses Juno, Pallas Athene and Venus.

Parrhasius: well known Greek painter.

Parthians: people living to east and north of today's Syria, famous for battleground manoeuvre of apparent retreat followed by rapid turn and arrow fire; after Roman defeat under Crassus 53 BC, they held Roman standards until return negotiated under Augustus; "Parthian river" is Euphrates;

Patara: sea port of Lycia in Asia Minor with oracle of Apollo.

Paulus: Lucius Aemilius Paulus, consul 219 and 216 BC; killed at Battle of Cannae 216 BC.

Paulus Maximus: Paulus Fabius Maximus; born c 46 BC; member of distinguished senatorial family in Rome; addressee of Odes IV.1 (c 16 BC); married Marcia first cousin of Augustus; consul 11 BC; governor of Asia 10 BC.

Pegasus: winged horse given by Minerva to Perseus; later carried Bellerophon.

Peleus: fled from Aegina to Iolcus where Acastus, thinking he had designs on his wife, challenged him to hunting contest; Peleus won with magic sword, which Acastus then hid, asking Centaurs to kill him but Cheiron saved him; see Hippolyte.

Pelops: son of Tantalus, founder of Atrides clan; father of Atreus and Thyestes, grandfather of Agamemnon and Menelaus; name given to Peloponnese (= island of Pelops).

Penates: Latin household gods (III.23); they and Lares (*qv*) were represented by small idols remaining in family if they moved home.

Penelope: wife of Odysseus, King of Ithaca; held off wooers for twenty years by never completing shroud she was weaving.

Pentheus: mythical king of Thebes who, clothed in animal skin, spied on the Bacchantes' celebrations and was torn apart by them.

Perseus: son of Jupiter and Danae, slayer of Gorgon, owner of Pegasus, husband of Andromeda.

Persian decoration: eastern costume adopted by Mark Antony and disparaged in Rome.

Phaethon: son of sun god Apollo, lost control of father's horses and destroyed by Jupiter to prevent destruction of earth.

Phalanthus: founder of Tarentum c 700 BC.

Phidyle: name of country girl (III.23)

Philippi: site in Macedonia near border of Thrace where decisive battle was fought between Caesarians and Brutus 42 BC; see Chapter 1.

Phocis: area of mainland Greece between Boeotia and Aetolia.

Pholoe: girl's name.

Phraates: Phraates IV of Parthia, hostile to Rome, enemy of Tiridates; ruled Parthia in 30s but lost his throne, recovering it 26 BC.

Phthia: town in Thessaly, birthplace of Achilles.

Phyllis: name of blond girlfriend of Xanthias (II.4); addressee of IV.11 ("do-re-mi" ode, see Chapters 2 and 3).

Pierian: adjective from Mount Pierus in Thessaly, sacred to Muses; see Pimplean.

Pimplean: spring near Mount Pierus sacred to Muses.

Pindar: (518–438 BC) born near Thebes in Boeotia; perhaps greatest Greek lyric poet, his odes were sung at Olympic, Pythian, Nemean and Isthmian Games.

Pindus: mountain home of Muses in Thessaly.

Pirithous: king of Lapiths who slew the Centaurs; husband of Hippodamia, after whose death he descended to underworld with Theseus and tried to abduct Proserpine; seized and put in chains.

Plancus: Munatius Plancus; addressee of I.7; veteran statesman who served under Julius Caesar and Mark Antony; consul 42 BC, year of battle of Philippi; as governor of Asia and Syria, joined Octavian 32 BC; proposed title of Augustus in Settlement of 27 BC; see Chapter 1.

Pleiades: daughters of Atlas and Pleione; constellation otherwise known as Seven Stars;

Pluto: God of Underworld and husband of Proserpina.

Pollio: Asinius Pollio; addressee of III.1; b 76 BC to senatorial family with interests in brick and tile manufacture; addressee of II.1; military service under Julius Caesar and Mark Antony in Gaul; at Brundisium 40 BC refused request from Antony's brother Lucius to attack Octavian's troops (see Chapter 1); consul 40 BC aged 36; triumph 39 BC after victory over Dalmatians; used booty to rebuild Atrium Libertatis as public library in Rome and amass statue collection; wrote History of the Civil Wars; addressee of Virgil's Fourth Eclogue.

Pollux: see Castor

Polyhymnia: Greek Muse of poetry and song.

Pompeius: addressee of II.7; probably Pompeius Varus; Horace's friend and comrade-in-arms at Philippi; not to be confused with Pompey the Great or Sextus Pompeius, see Chapter 1.

Pompilius: second king of Rome.

Porphyrion: giant who rebelled against Jupiter.

Postumus: addressee of II.14; possibly senator Propertius Postumus, who left wife Aelia Galla to go to eastern wars.

Praeneste: hill town east of Rome, today's Palestrina; site of several senatorial estates, including a summer house of Augustus.

Priam: King of Troy, husband of Hecuba and father of Troilus in Trojan War.

Primus: Marcus Primus; proconsul of Macedonia, found guilty in 23 BC of attacking Thrace without senatorial authority, see Chapter 1.

Procne: daughter of Pandion of Athens and descendant of Cecrops; tongue cut out by husband Tereus, who seduced her sister Philomela; she boiled her son Itys in a cauldron and fed him to Tereus; turned into a swallow by gods; see Itys and Tereus.

Proconsul: Roman rank of one who has served as consul, then becoming governor of overseas province.

Proculeius: Caius Proculeius, knight; friend of Augustus; half-brother of Maecenas's wife Terentia and Murena; reference to his brothers (II.2) is not to Licinius but two full brothers.

Procyon: major star of Lesser Dog, which rose before Dog Star itself.

Prometheus: formed men of clay and animated them with fire stolen from heaven; for his punishment, see II.13.

Proserpina: Queen of Underworld and wife of Pluto; her duties included cutting lock of hair from dead.

Proteus: sea god who served Neptune.

Proteus: mythical king of Tiryns; his wife Anteia fell in love with Bellerophon, who rejected her advances; she told Proteus he had tried to seduce her, whereupon he sent Bellerophon with letter to Anteia's father Iobates king of Lycia requiring his death; see Bellerophon.

Punic: Phoenician; often synonymous with Carthaginian.

Pyrrha: wife of Deucalion, known for flood sent by Jupiter; not connected with subject of I.5.

Pyrrhus: king of Epirus; invaded Italy 280 BC; also name of friend of Horace (III.20).

Pythagoras: son of Panthous; b Samos c 550 BC; mathematician, philosopher and musical scientist; studied in Egypt and Babylon, before founding school at Croton in southern Italy.

Pythian: adjective for Delphi, where Apollo killed python.

Quinctius: see Hirpinus.

Quintilius: mourned in I.24; possibly Quintilius Varus, *qv*.

Quirinus: name given to Romulus.

Raeti: tribe of mouintainous region north of River Po, between rivers Danube, Rhine and Lech; defeated by Tiberius fifteen years after fall of Alexandria.

Regulus: Marcus Atilius Regulus, consul with Manlius Vulso 256 BC in First Punic War; beat off Carthaginian naval threat against Sicily at battle of Cape Ecnomus; invaded Africa, defeated at Bagradas; sent back to Rome on parole to negotiate Sicilian settlement, advised against compromise, returning voluntarily to captors; subject of III.5.

Rhadamanthus: judge of shades of the dead.

Rhode: girl's name (two syllables).

Rhodes: island off coast of Asia Minor.

Rhoetus: giant participating in revolt against Jupiter.

Roman Odes: name given to first six odes of Book III.

Romulus: grandson of Juno, son of Mars and Rhea Silvia, mythical founder of Rome; Juno let him escape death by flying to heaven on Mars' horses (III.3).

Sabine Hills: site near Tibur where Horace's farmhouse, given by Maecenas, was situated, together with five tenant farms.

Sacred Way (*Via Sacra*): road leading into Rome from east towards Capitol and forming part of triumphal route.

Salamis: island off southern coast of Attica.

Salians: "Leapers," religious college of priests dedicated to service of Mars and known for lively dancing around holy places, especially in first half of March.

Sallustius: see Crispus.

Sappho: 7th century BC lyric poetess from Lesbos; model for Horace's Sapphic metre.

Scauri: distinguished Roman family, holding consulships in 115 and 108 BC.

Scipio: Publius Cornelius Scipio Africanus: brought Second Punic War to decisive end at Battle of Zama 202 BC, for which surnamed Africanus.

Scopas: well-known Greek sculptor.

Scythians: nomadic people roaming steppes of today's Ukraine and beyond.

Senate and the People of Rome: SPQR (*Senatus Populusque Romanus*), official title of Roman republic with initials shown on Roman military standards.

Septimius: addressee of II.6; perhaps the mutual friend Septimius referred to in letter by Augustus quoted by Suetonius in biography of Horace.

Sestius: Lucius Sestius, addressee of First Spring Ode, I.4; former *quaestor* to Marcus Brutus, but appointed consul to replace Augustus after crisis of 23 BC.

Sheba: country in region of today's Yemen.

Sibylline Books: responsibility of the Fifteen Men (college of priests); contained collection of prophetic verses bearing on Roman policy and religion, often originating with the Sibyl at Cumae, prophetess in service of Apollo; the Books divided time into cycles of 110 years.

Sicily, Sea of: site of Roman naval victories in First Punic War 264–241 BC; see also Palinurus.

Silvan: god of forests and thickets, otherwise Silvanus.

Simonides: (c 554–466 BC) b island of Ceos, Greek lyric poet, famed for songs in honour of dead.

Sisyphus: prince of Corinth killed by Theseus; his punishment was to push rock uphill in underworld, only for it always to roll back down again.

Sithone: town in Thrace, birthplace of Horace's friend Chloe.

Soracte: mountain in Etruria, north of Rome.

Spartacus: leader of slave rebellion of 73–71 BC.

Spring Odes: I.4 (First Spring Ode) and IV.7 (Second Spring Ode).

Sthenelus: Greek hero (I.14, IV.9), charioteer of Diomede at siege of Troy, occupant of Wooden Horse.

Styx: river crossed by Charon's ferry carrying dead to reach underworld.

Sulpicius: wine merchant.

Sybaris: male name associated with city noted for effeminate and lax behaviour; see Thurium.

Sygambri: powerful German tribe living between today's rivers Sieg and Ruhr as far as the Lippe.

Syrtes: sand banks off north coast of today's Morocco.

Tanais: today's River Don.

Tantalus: father of Pelops; revealed secrets of gods after dining with them; punished by being unable to reach fruit above head or water under chin, suffering eternal hunger and thirst.

Tarentum: originally Spartan settlement in southern Italy, founded by Phalanthus; birthplace of Archytas.

Tarquin: fifth king of Rome.

Tecmessa: daughter of King Teuthras; mistress of Ajax.

Telegonus: son of Odysseus and Circe, not to be confused with Telemachus; sailed for Ithaca in search of father; mistaking it for Corcyra, attacked Odysseus, killing him with spear tipped with sting-ray's spine; later founded Tusculum in Alban Hills.

Telemachus: son of Odysseus and Penelope; prince of Ithaca.

Telemon: father of Ajax.

Telephus: addressee of I.13 and III.19, and named in IV.11.

Tempe: Thessalian valley and beauty spot.

Teos: birthplace of Greek lyric poet Anacreon.

Terentia: wife of Maecenas, sister of Murena; see Licymnia and Chapter 1.

Tereus: husband of Procne, father of Itys, seduced wife's sister Philomela, imprisoned Procne and cut out her tongue, but Philomela released her; Procne killed Itys and fed him to Tereus; he planned to axe sisters to death, but gods changed Procne to swallow, Philomela to nightingale and Tereus to hoopoe.

Teucer: banished son of Telamon, king of Sparta.

Thalia: a Muse.

Thaliarchus: Greek for "Master of Festivities" (I.9) perhaps major domo or friend chosen by lot to lead drinking party (*symposium*).

Thebes: city of Greece; site of dragon slain by king Cadmus ordered by Athene to sew its teeth; armed men sprang up, but Cadmus tricked them into fighting among themselves and Echion was one of five survivors; later Thebes was target of Seven Against Thebes; see Amphiaraus and Amphion.

Theseus: mythical king of Athens, lover of Ariadne whom he abandoned, father of Hipplolytus (son of the Amazon Hippolyte), husband of Phaedra; killer of Sisyphus and the Minotaur, friend of Pirithous.

Thessaly: region of northern Greece west of Bosporus and adjoining Macedonia.

Thetis: mother of Achilles.

Thurium: Thurii, city of Lucania on Gulf of Tarentum on site of ancient Sybaris; name varied to create rhyme (III.9).

Thyestes: son of Pelops; served up to his brother Atreus the flesh of his son.

Tiber: river of Rome, called "yellow" by Horace because of the colour of its soil.

Tiberius: (42 BC–37 AD) stepson of Augustus, daughter of his second wife Livia, *qv*; military achievements in Germany (IV.14); succeeded Augustus as emperor.

Tibullus: contemporary of Horace, addressee of I.33; Roman poet sponsored by Corvinus; died 19 BC aged about 35.

Tibur: town east of Rome near Horace's farmhouse, today's Tivoli; founded by Tiburtus of Argos; site of senatorial mansions, including one of Augustus.

Tigris: river flowing through Parthian empire.

Tiridates: prince of Parthia; supported by Augustus, hostile to Phraates IV, twice taking refuge in Rome.

Titans: giants supported by Saturn father of Jupiter in their revolt against Jupiter.

Tithonus: consort of Aurora, goddess of dawn, granted immortality and turned into cicada.

Tityos: giant, son of Jupiter; tried to seduce Lato; punished by being stretched out in underworld where vulture fed incessantly on his liver.

Torquatus: Lucius Manlius Torquatus, consul 65 BC, year of Horace's birth (III.21).

Torquatus: Torquatus Manlius; addressee of Second Spring Ode, IV.7; last known member of Manlius clan, several members having been killed in civil wars; Epicurean; did not seek political honours.

Troilus: son of King Priam of Troy and Hecuba; killed by Achilles in Trojan War.

Tullus: see Volcacius.

Tullus: third of legendary kings of ancient Rome.

Tydeus: father of Diomedes.

Typhoeus: giant killed by Jupiter's thunderbolt and buried under Mount Etna.

Ulysses: Greek name for Odysseus.

Ustica: hilly area near Horace's Sabine farm.

Valgius: Caius Valgius Rufus; addressee of II.9; scholar, elegiac poet, writer of uncompleted work on medicinal plants, member of circle of Messalla Corvinus; substitute consul 12 BC.

Varus: addressee of I.18; possibly the Quintilius Varus mourned in I.24, referred to in Horace's Art of Poetry (lines 438–444); see also Pompeius.

243

Varius: Lucius Varius Rufus; epic poet and tragedian; friend of Augustus; Epicurean; contemporary of Horace.

Venafrum: town in Campania.

Venus: Greek Aphrodite, goddess of love.

Venusia: birthplace of Horace in province of Apulia.

Vesta: alternative name for Cybele, earth mother or *Magna Mater* identified with fertility.

Vindelici: German tribe based on today's Augsburg.

Virgil: Publius Vergilius Maro; addressee of I.3 and I.24 (possible but uncertain addressee of IV.12); author of *Eclogues, Georgics* and *Aeneid*, sponsored by Maecenas; died 19 BC.

Volcacius: Lucius Volcacius Tullus, consul 66 BC; son of same name was consul in 33 BC.

Voltur: mountain, five miles west of Venusia, where settlements of Forentum, Bantia and Acherontia were situated.

Vulcan: fire god, son of Jupiter and Juno.

Xanthias of Phocis: addressee of II.4.

Xanthus: river in Lycia.